THE ONE MINUTE COACH TO MASTERING YOUR EMOTIONS

THE ONE MINUTE COACH TO MASTERING YOUR EMOTIONS

A Step-by-Step Guide to Feeling Happy on a Regular Basis

Masha Malka

Published by
Hybrid Global Publishing
301 E 57th Street, 4th fl
New York, NY 10022

Copyright © 2017 by Masha Malka

All rights reserved. No part of this book may be reproduced or transmitted in any form or by any means, electronic or mechanical, including photocopying, recording, or by any information storage and retrieval system, without the written permission of the Publisher, except where permitted by law.

Manufactured in the United States of America, or in the
United Kingdom when distributed elsewhere.

Malka, Masha
The One Minute Coach to Mastering Your Emotions: A Step-by-Step Guide to Feeling Happy on a Regular Basis
LCCN: 2017961441
ISBN: 978-1-938015-90-8
eBook: 978-1-938015-91-5

Cover design: Anna Polosky
Cover photo: MeramarIMAGES
Editing: Michael Bowker
Interior design: Medlar Publishing Solutions Pvt Ltd., India
Artwork: Anna Polonsky

www.mashamalka.com
www.theoneminutecoachbooks.com

TABLE OF CONTENTS

Forward by Michael Bowker ix
Introduction to Mastering Your Emotions xi
    All Emotions are a Purely Human Experience xii
    How This Book is Structured and Why xiv

Part 1: Getting to Know Your Emotions – Getting to Know You

Chapter 1	What Do You Really Want?	2
Chapter 2	Why Knowing What You Don't Want Can Be an Asset	4
Chapter 3	Your Energy and Your Vibrations	6
Chapter 4	How to Raise the Energetic Frequency	8
Chapter 5	Raising Your Vibration through Your Environment	10
Chapter 6	Raising Your Vibration through Your Thoughts and Emotions	12
Chapter 7	What is Stopping You from Taking Action Based on What You Know?	14
Chapter 8	Learning to Love Myself	16
Chapter 9	Are You an Expert at Surviving?	18
Chapter 10	What Do You Believe In and Why?	20
Chapter 11	Self-Fulfilling Prophesy	22
Chapter 12	Your Physical Body	24
Chapter 13	Your Emotional Body	26
Chapter 14	Your Mental Body	28

Part 2: Emotions that Cause Us Pain and Suffering

Chapter 15	Why Do We Suffer?	32
Chapter 16	The Pain of Fear and Resistance	34
Chapter 17	My Caving Adventure and What It Taught Me	36
Chapter 18	The Pain of Grief and Despair	40

Chapter 19	The Pain of Missing Someone	42
Chapter 20	The Pain of Feeling Guilt and Shame	44
Chapter 21	The Pain of Resentment and How to Forgive	46
Chapter 22	The Pain of Not Feeling in Control	48
Chapter 23	The Pain of Failure	50
Chapter 24	The Pain of Feeling Insignificant, Unimportant, and Not Needed	52
Chapter 25	The Pain of Anger and Resentment	54
Chapter 26	The Pain of Jealousy in a Relationship	56
Chapter 27	The Pain of Doubt and Worry	58
Chapter 28	The Pain of Anxiety	60
Chapter 29	The Pain of Feeling Overwhelmed and Discouraged	62
Chapter 30	The Pain of Disappointment	64
Chapter 31	The Pain of Feeling Frustrated, Irritated, and Impatient	66
Chapter 32	The Pain of Boredom	68
Chapter 33	Avoiding Disappointments and Arguments	70

Part 3: Understand and Boost Your Feel-Good Emotions

Chapter 34	Choosing to Feel Good on a Regular Basis	74
Chapter 35	The Pleasure of Feeling Healthy	76
Chapter 36	The Pleasure of Feeling Confident	78
Chapter 37	The Pleasure of Feeling Valued	80
Chapter 38	The Pleasure of Being in a Loving Relationship	82
Chapter 39	The Pleasure of Feeling Connected	84
Chapter 40	The Pleasure of Feeling Free	86
Chapter 41	The Pleasure of Feeling Prosperous and Abundant	88
Chapter 42	The Pleasure of Feeling Beautiful	90
Chapter 43	The Pleasure of Feeling Happy	92
Chapter 44	The Pleasure of Feeling Peace of Mind	94
Chapter 45	The Pleasure of Feeling Gratitude	96

Part 4: Mastering Your Emotions – Mastering Your Life

Chapter 46	What Does it Mean to Master Your Emotions?	100
Chapter 47	You Are Not Your Story	102
Chapter 48	How to Free Yourself from the Stories Which Don't Serve You Anymore	104
Chapter 49	How and Why We Filter Our Reality	106
Chapter 50	How to Consciously Program Yourself	108
Chapter 51	Five Rules of Mind Programing for Affirmations, Goals and Vision Writing	110
	Present Tense	110
	Personal	110
	Positive	110
	Precise and Repeated Regularly	110
	Use Emotion	111
Chapter 52	I Like Myself	112
Chapter 53	I Am One	114
Chapter 54	The Dangerous Habit of Thinking	116
Chapter 55	Meditation Made Easy	118
Chapter 56	A Word on Hypnosis	120
Chapter 57	Stop the Drama	122
Chapter 58	Just Be Yourself	124
Chapter 59	Releasing Guilt	126
Chapter 60	Awareness Doesn't Always Produce the Results	128
Chapter 61	Life without Challenges	130
Chapter 62	How to Break the Pattern of a Persistent Emotion	132
Chapter 63	Dealing with an Emotional Crisis	134
Chapter 64	Be the Light	136
Chapter 65	Patience is a Virtue	138

Part 5: Conclusion

Chapter 66	The Dance of Life	142
Chapter 67	When Sh-t Happens	144

Chapter 68	The Danger of Desire	146
Chapter 69	The Importance of Humility	148
Chapter 70	The Formula for Living a Good Life	150
Conclusion	Tomorrow Is Promised to No One	152
Appendix I	Ten Basic Steps for Releasing Emotions	*154*
Appendix II	Holistic Approach to Identifying and Releasing Five Most Common Unwanted Emotions	*156*
	Anger	156
	Sorrow/Sadness	158
	Worry	159
	Grief	161
	Fear	162
About the Artist		*164*
About the Author		*165*
Personal Message		*166*

FORWARD

by Michael Bowker

(Author of *Playing from the Heart, Fatal Deception, Gods of Our Time* and others. Former contributor to the *Los Angeles Times*.)

Several months ago I received an email from a writer in Spain, who was referred to me by a mutual colleague in New Zealand. It was through this global route that the gifted writer who lives in Spain, but who is actually a Russian/American, Masha Malka, first contacted me at my office in Santa Barbara, California.

She asked me to edit her newest book, and I wondered how that might work out. Masha and I come from vastly different cultures. She spent her childhood in the Soviet Union and lived all over the world before settling in a beautiful part of southern Spain. I grew up on a hard, little farm in Kansas before immigrating to California – she has never seen Kansas, and although I have done publishing deals in Kiev, I have never seen the Black Sea or the Carpathian Mountains. It didn't seem like a likely partnership, at first.

Then I read Masha's first draft of *The One Minute Coach to Mastering Your Emotions*, and it quickly became clear to me that she had captured universal human truths though beautifully written stories. She transcends cultures and moves to the common heart of us all in this book. She writes with great clarity and sincerity. Through my career as a writer, editor and publisher, I've read scores of self-help books, and none of them inspire or impress me more that this book.

We had to learn to dance together, at first, because Masha has a special style and a feminine strength that took me a moment to gather and feel its rhythms. It didn't take long, though, before I 'got it' and joined with her in the book's special flow and powerful grace.

This is a 'smart' book. It is a book from the heart, but most of all, it is a book that teaches us how to gain control of our lives by understanding and mastering our emotions. Masha's delivery is simple, but her messages, insights and action steps may profoundly change your life. She is candid about the events of her own life that helped lead her to these insights, and she shares them in an intimate and friendly way.

But, make no mistake, you will probably never be the same after reading this book and you will be happier for it. You'll probably laugh a lot more and feel better about yourself and your life. I am proud to have played a small role in helping Masha with this book.

I think you'll find it worth every 'minute' you spend reading it. It is a remarkable book that crosses all boundaries and cultures. She writes that, "There is *beauty* in all emotions," and I think you will agree with me that there is also beauty inside these pages.

INTRODUCTION

TO MASTERING YOUR EMOTIONS

Did you know that even though people have been living and feeling for thousands of years, they only started labelling and categorizing emotions less than 200 years ago? Moreover, not all cultures use the same labels and categories and there is a wide range of emotions for which we have no name.

No wonder it is difficult for us to express how we feel, not just to others, but also to ourselves. Because a large chunk of our communication is done through words, if there are no words to describe something, we become like toddlers, knowing that we want something, not being able to express it, and getting angry and frustrated because of it.

Let me ask you, how many emotions can you name? How many of the ones that you can think of are the emotions that you would consider feel-good or pleasant emotions and how many that would make you feel uneasy, and bring you discomfort or pain?

In her bestselling book – *The Book of Human Emotions*, Tiffany Watt Smith talks about 55 emotions she researched and collected from different times and cultures. Her list was equally divided between those emotions we welcome and those we would prefer to avoid. However, it is important to keep in mind that in our own lives, emotions are not so neatly balanced. It is the *emotions we express most often and pay most attention to every day that are predominantly present in our lives.*

Recently I went to a famous art gallery in London and found a huge majority of the art work depicting suffering, rivalry, violence, and natural disasters rather than peaceful and beautiful landscapes or attractive happy people. Why is that?

Why does the media focuses a huge majority of its attention on negative and distractive news that makes us feel enraged, sad, angry, upset, fearful, and diverts our focus to how unfair and dangerous this world is; even though there are just as many kind, beautiful, and heartwarming stories out there?

The easiest way to manipulate someone is to make them feel a certain way and we are manipulated constantly to buy, to do, and to accept something that serves the interests of someone else and not us.

Becoming aware of what you are feeling on a regular basis and at every moment can prevent you from being a zombie and can put you back in control of your emotions, your life and the quality of its experience.

If you are tired of being a slave to your emotions, allowing them to run your life, then realize that you don't have to anymore.

In this book you will learn how to master your emotions, make them your friends, and understand the messages that they bring to help you grow, expand and get in touch with your true self.

Yes, every emotion has its place and its reason for being; however, what we do with those emotions is what needs to be mastered.

ALL EMOTIONS ARE A PURELY HUMAN EXPERIENCE

In 2001 I had, what many would call, an out of body experience...

I have rarely talked about what happened to me that day. For many years I didn't tell a soul until I attended a seminar held by a best-selling author, entrepreneur, and philanthropist Amyn Daya, who opened his seminar by sharing *his* near-death, out-of-body experience.

Somewhere on the 5th row, I sat frozen, listening to him describe how what should have been a fatal motorcycle accident, ended up leaving his bike in pieces, but him without a scratch on his body. What he described was almost exactly what I experienced a few years back! Hearing his story and how drastically it changed his life gave me the courage to share mine.

It was late in the evening in 2001, and my baby girl was fast asleep, which gave me a chance to sit at my computer and catch up on some work. I was feeling tired. Not so much physically as emotionally.

A few years back my husband and I moved from Miami to Europe in search of a perfect place to start a family. After briefly living in Vienna and London, and visiting many other cities, we found that perfect place in a beautiful town called Marbella, in the south of Spain.

At the time, I was totally in love with my husband and without realizing it, I made a mistake of making him the center of my existence and didn't make any close friends in the new country. When my baby was born, I felt complete, happy, and fulfilled and thought that my dream had come true and I had succeeded in life.

So when my husband announced to me, completely unexpectedly, that he decided to leave me, I felt my perfect little world fall apart and I went to pieces emotionally. I felt so alone. I was too heartbroken or maybe too embarrassed to tell anyone. After all, I thought, if I couldn't keep my marriage together, I was a total failure! I know now it was immature for me to feel that way, but at that time, I couldn't face telling anyone about it, especially my family. "What if they won't like me either?" I thought, filled with insecurity, doubt, and, for some reason, guilt.

In that state of despair and deep loneliness, tired of the overpowering emotions within myself and not being able to talk to anyone, I put my head down on my hands, and the next thing I felt was myself rising above my body. I could see my body motionless sitting at my desk with my head down on my hands as I rose higher and then saw two huge clouds shaped like hands which gently enveloped me.

The minute I left my body all the pain stopped! I felt nothing other than a complete peace and the kind of love that is difficult to describe. It is difficult to describe because it wasn't really a feeling, it was a state of being.

What I found very intriguing was that the love I felt for my baby or for my husband or for my mother or for anyone human was not felt any more. I was especially surprised when it came to my baby because 'back on earth', I felt she was my everything, my reason for existence, my dream-come-true…and here I was, up in the clouds, not feeling any of it!

I heard the Voice and the Voice said, *"You are never alone!"* After a conversation that I can't recall in detail now, another message was clear – *"You are always safe."*

The break from the pain was truly welcoming and the deep peace, love, and the lack of any other emotions that keep us living in fear of death were absent.

As 'The Hands' started to gently take me down, I asked if I could stay. The Voice said that my mission was not over and that I had a lot of work left to do and yet, I knew that I could choose. I chose to go back but, as anyone who had the blessing of experiencing what it feels like in that other dimension, life could never be the same again. The first reconnection I made was with my daughter. I was overjoyed to feel that I felt a deeper bond with her than ever.

What I took with me from that experience was this:

1. I am never alone.
2. I am safe.
3. Death is not scary.
4. ALL emotions are a purely human experience. The soul only feels peace and profound all-encompassing love.

And this is the reason why this book came about. *I have learned that we are here to experience.* Not to learn, not to grow, not to become better, not to achieve some deeds or fix some karma… At our core, we are already perfect.

We are here to experience. Experience life, in ALL its aspects, without judgement.

And the way we experience being a human is through *emotions*.

This means that if you can understand how to master your emotions, disassociate from them, and work with them rather than push them away, or get swallowed by them, you can then navigate your life to have the kind of experiences that your soul desires.

You can learn to use your emotions to be your guides and your friends and understand how perfectly you are designed when your emotions, your body, and your mind work harmoniously together.

HOW THIS BOOK IS STRUCTURED AND WHY

This book is part of *The One Minute Coach* series of books – books that are designed for:

- Smart and busy people who often don't have the time to read, even if they would love to;
- People who don't just want the information, they want to know what to do with it;
- People who understand that the value of a good book is not in how complicated or fancy the words are in it or how thick the book is, but by how much

their time invested in reading it gives them a return on that investment based on *how the quality of their life improves* during and after they read it.

The book is written using the rules of the *Accelerated Learning Techniques,* which emphasize the use of both right and left hemispheres of the brain for faster and easier learning and later recollection.

Each chapter in this book takes about a minute to read and each chapter is followed by action steps explaining what you can do with the information you just read. This is because I believe that there is already an information overload and what people need is not more information but *an understanding of what to do with it.*

The image at the end of each chapter helps with the whole brain learning and recollection. It also makes it more fun to read. I always wondered why only kids should have fun books with images, so I decided if I ever write a book, it would have images in it.

There are five parts to this book. The first part introduces you to the world of emotions and helps you see them from a different perspective. The second part focuses on the feel-bad emotions and the third part on the feel-good emotions. The forth part gives you practical tools for mastering your emotions and the fifth part helps you put it all together and integrate your new knowledge into your daily lives.

So, let me ask you a question, with which all change starts to happen… *Are you ready?*

If your answer is a "YES", let's begin!

PART 1

GETTING TO KNOW YOUR EMOTIONS— GETTING TO KNOW YOU

CHAPTER 1

WHAT DO YOU REALLY WANT?

Most of us are looking for true love… But what is love? Most of us are looking for happiness; yet, have you ever thought about what happiness is? Most of us want to achieve success, but what does it really mean to be successful? Even being healthy is a relative term.

Experiencing happiness, love, health, success, joy, freedom, passion, and anything else you might desire begins with a clear understanding of what each of them mean to YOU.

This is not something we tend to think about on a daily basis or ever. Henry Ford has been quoted saying,

"Thinking is the hardest work there is, which is probably the reason why so few engage in it."

Yet, if we are too lazy to direct our thoughts consciously in the direction we want them to go, we will most likely end up thinking thoughts on an unconscious level, creating a reality we don't really want to experience.

The reason for this is that our thoughts trigger certain emotions and those emotions determine the quality of our life in the present moment, and therefore, in our future and our overall experience of life.

Action Steps

- Think about the emotions you experience on a regular basis and write them down. Now look at your list and decide which of these emotions you rather not experience anymore and which you would like to experience more often?
- According to your list, do you tend to mostly worry, feel frustrated, irritated, impatient, insecure, angry, disappointed, judgmental, or overwhelmed or do you mostly experience emotions such as love, confidence, freedom, joy, vitality, gratitude, inner peace, contentment, respect, creativity, success, appreciation, excitement, fulfilment, and faith?
- Now feel for a moment what your life would be like if you could experience all of your feel-good emotions on a regular basis? Would the experience of your life be different to the one you are living now? How eager would you be to get up in the morning and to start your day? More eager than now?
- All you need is enough desire to make a change and then to follow through with the action steps in this book and watch your life transform and adopt to the new you!

CHAPTER 2

WHY KNOWING WHAT YOU DON'T WANT CAN BE AN ASSET

More often than not, people do not really know what they want, though they can easily make a list of everything they would rather *not* experience any more. This can be an asset as well as a liability.

It is an asset because much of what we want is often defined by first understanding what we don't want – what makes us unhappy, uncomfortable, and goes against our true nature. This is the reason why teenagers experiment so much, making, what seems like many mistakes in the process, where in fact, they are testing their boundaries while learning who they are – what works for them and what doesn't.

It can be a liability because if we spend too much time focusing on what we don't want and what doesn't work, we often create more of it.

So there comes a time when it is important to take what you don't want and make it work for you – reverse it, focusing on the opposite and on what you *do* want and what would make you happy.

The best way to think of what you want is by focusing on the *final outcome* and not the means to getting there. For example, most likely, it is not lots of money that you want, it is what that money can buy for you AND how you would *feel* when that happens. So money becomes the means to the final outcome, which might be experiencing a sense of security or a feeling of success.

Understanding what you don't want any more is the first step in knowing what you do want. But be careful – always focus on the final outcome of what you desire. And your final outcome is always your emotions and your general state of being.

Action Steps

- If you woke up tomorrow and a miracle had taken place – what you most desire had happened, what emotions would you be experiencing that would reveal to you that miracle had happened?
- Answering this question will help you outline your desired state of being. Emerging yourself into that state as often as possible will help you attract more and more of the same emotions without you controlling the process or the means of getting there.

Don't want   *Want*

CHAPTER 3

YOUR ENERGY AND YOUR VIBRATIONS

It is difficult for us to conceptualize the fact that we are and everything around us is energy. On the other hand, spending time contemplating difficult concepts is not necessary in order to use the knowledge to our advantage.

What is important to understand is that everything around you has a particular energetic charge and energetic vibration. Each emotion, each food you eat, each thought you think, the sound of someone's voice, the words you hear, the trees, the flowers, animals, even buildings and cities – all have a particular vibration.

Think about what you want to manifest because it also has a particular energetic vibration and in order for you to be successful in manifesting what you want, you need to vibrate on that same frequency.

Simply put, the more positive and feel-good your emotions and experiences are, the higher their vibrational frequency. In order to manifest what you want, and I assume what you want is something positive that feels good, you need to raise your energetic frequency, constantly.

When I ask my little boy about his day in school, the usual answer is, do you want the good news first or the bad news? I usually ask for the bad news first, leaving the best for last. So the bad news here is that even to maintain your energetic vibration as it is right now, you have to work on it because naturally, it tends to go down.

Feeling good and staying positive requires effort, just as it requires effort to stay physically and mentally fit and agile. The good news is that after the initial effort, knowing what to do and keeping the vibration high becomes habitual and practically automatic.

Some people get into the routine or a habit of brushing their teeth and taking a shower every morning; some people get into the routine of playing tennis or football or going to the gym on certain days at certain times; and some people get into the routine of conscious creation and positive vibration. Some, of course, do all three and more. It is always a choice.

Action Steps

- Feeling good is a choice.
- You might not choose (at least not consciously) what happens to you or around you but you can always choose how you *react* to it.
- Refuse to create drama in your life and choose to see the best in each situation.
- Decide that for the next 24 hours you will not get disappointed, judgmental, frustrated, or angry with anything.
- Accept everything as is and look for what is good about it. Even 24 hours of such conscious living can change your life exponentially.

CHAPTER 4

HOW TO RAISE THE ENERGETIC FREQUENCY

As we discussed in the previous chapter, everything around you has a particular energetic vibration. In order for you to attract the people and opportunities that will leave you feeling good, you need to "vibrate" at the same frequency, as if tuning in to that particular radio station.

To do that, you need to first become conscious of the energies you surround yourself with, or put inside of yourself, and you can consciously choose to keep your vibration high.

The basic four things to pay attention to when raising your frequency are:

- Breathing
- Food
- Environment
- Thoughts and Emotions

Breathing fills your Being with oxygen, rejuvenates your organs and your every cell, and feeds your brain. It also helps you raise your vibration and allows you to remain centered and connected.

Food, like everything else around us, also has energy and by putting food inside yourself, you make that energy a part of you. If you put, what I call, dead food into your body – food that is heavily processed, fried, or comes from dead animals – it will affect you differently than the food that is alive, such as fresh vegetables and fruits.

Your environment, which includes the people with whom you surround yourself, as well as your physical location, also play big roles in the quality of your vibration.

However, it is your thoughts and emotions which play the most important role in the quality of your energetic vibration and the quality of life that you are experiencing right now.

How to Raise the Energetic Frequency | 9

> **Action Steps**
>
> - If there is something in your life right now that you don't like, ask yourself who or what in your environment might be bringing your vibration down. Pay attention to what you eat; what you are thinking and feeling on a regular basis, the words you regularly use, and how much oxygen you are getting.
> - For example, the best ways to get more oxygen into your body is by drinking enough water, getting enough exercise, and learning how to breathe correctly.
> - Also, make an effort to eat more food that is alive and not processed. The more processed the food, the lower the vibration and you are making it a part of you.
> - In the next two chapters, we will explore how your environment and how your thoughts and emotions affect your energetic vibration.

CHAPTER 5

RAISING YOUR VIBRATION THROUGH YOUR ENVIRONMENT

In this book, I define your 'environment' as your home, workplace, city and the country in which you live. I also include the people you choose to have around you.

Most of you have probably heard of *Feng Shui*, the Chinese-based philosophy of how energy flows in our personal environments. I am a fan of its concepts and of the blueprint it provides for manipulating our immediate environment to our practical and emotional advantage. I recommend browsing through some of the books focusing on this valuable and powerful concept.

We might not always be able to immediately choose our city, country, workplace, or even our homes; however, with the awareness and the knowledge of a few rules, we can make our immediate environment as pleasant and as uplifting as possible. This choice is vital because if something in our environment is bothering us, it will keep driving our energy down.

Eventually, when manifesting what you want becomes your second nature, choosing where you live and what is around you becomes easier and so does making your environment a nurturing, happy place.

The second part of our environment that affects the quality of our energetic vibration includes the people who surround us. Every person vibrates a particular frequency and unfortunately, the lower frequency would, more often than not, bring the higher frequency down to match theirs. Therefore, it is very important to choose friends carefully.

Action Steps

- Clear the energy of your home and your workplace by getting rid of the clutter and re-arranging your furniture in a pleasing way.
- Do not be afraid to throw away what is old or not used on a regular basis. *You cannot attract something new while you are holding on to the old.*
- Now add some elements that make your environment joyful and pleasant and reflect your personality.
- When you allow someone to drain you of energy, you basically disrespect yourself by putting their interests ahead of yours. Surround yourself with positive, supportive, and uplifting people who are genuinely happy for your successes, don't judge you for your actions, and accept you as you are.

CHAPTER 6

RAISING YOUR VIBRATION THROUGH YOUR THOUGHTS AND EMOTIONS

Each of our thoughts and emotions also corresponds to different vibrational frequencies. It is logical that the lower the vibration of the thought, the lower the vibration of the emotion it attracts, and the worse we feel.

The movies and the TV programs we watch, the music that we listen to, the books, magazines, or newspapers that we read – ALL affect how we feel and all program us on a deep subconscious level.

When the low frequency thoughts and emotions settle in within our conscience, we start to attract people and circumstances that vibrate in the same low vibration. That is why when one bad thing happens, other bad things often tend to follow.

The same is true of course, when the vibration of our thoughts and emotions is high. The higher the vibration, the better is the experience of our life – unexpected fortune visits us, we win something, we meet someone amazing, we are asked to be a part of an exciting project, people are unusually polite to us, and we notice the amazing beauty that surrounds us. The list is endless.

Raising Your Vibration through Your Thoughts and Emotions | 13

Action Steps

- First, become aware of your thoughts on a regular basis as well as your habitual emotional reactions.
- Now, get a rubber band and put it on your wrist. Every time a negative or self-destructive thought comes into your head, pull that rubber band and let it go so that it snaps your wrist. This is one way to create awareness and to reprogram yourself to raise your thinking and emotional responses out of the subconscious realm, and into your consciousness.
- Choose carefully what you watch, listen to and read. Notice how it makes you feel.
- Be in control of what you allow to enter your mind and program it with positive affirmations, uplifting positive music, and positive actions that move your life forward.

CHAPTER 7

WHAT IS STOPPING YOU FROM TAKING ACTION BASED ON WHAT YOU KNOW?

It is always good to learn new things, but knowledge in itself is not power, as we often hear people say.

For example, knowing what to eat and how often to exercise, but not doing these things is not powerful at all. In fact, it just makes most of us feel guilty and adds to our stress levels, which in turn makes most of us gain more weight. This goes for all areas of our lives where we know what we 'should be' doing, but for various reasons don't.

So, if you have the knowledge, what is stopping you from taking positive action? Is it lack of motivation caused by fear of failure or pain of the unknown? Lack of time? Old, bad habits? Well, to some degree it might be all of the above but those are not the underlying true reasons.

Can you think of people who actually ARE motivated, not lazy, not scared, just as busy, to do what you feel you should be doing and they manage to do it, but you do not? Do you think they are in any way better than you? Of course not.

So what is the difference? Maybe they have stronger willpower? Or maybe they are just born different? Also not!

There is just ONE thing that is different…

People who are motivated, who overcome fear to create new and positive habits, and who find the time and the willpower to live the life consistent with their ideals simply LOVE THEMSELVES more than those who are still struggling.

However, it is one thing to have the knowledge and to understand and even believe that this is the case and it's a whole other thing *to know* what to do with this knowledge.

Action Steps

- First, remind yourself that if you are not following through with your goals or acting on what you know, it is not because you are not good enough, strong enough, lucky enough, etc., it is because deep down you don't feel that you *deserve a better quality of life*.
- Understanding the above statement will help you take more appropriate actions and will prevent unnecessary destructive emotions and thoughts.
- Second, learning to love and accept yourself unconditionally just as you are is a process and it takes time and effort. Throughout this book, many action steps will be designed to raise your level of self-esteem, self-love, and self-acceptance.

Here are some things you can do right away:

- Refuse to criticize yourself no matter what happens.
- Say "I love you!" as you look deeply into your eyes every morning, evening or every time you pass a mirror.
- When you do something disappointing and you are tempted to get upset with yourself, immediately go to the mirror and say, *"I love you no matter what!"*

CHAPTER 8

LEARNING TO LOVE MYSELF

I understood the concept of the importance of self-love for many years before I actually learned to apply this knowledge in a way that it made a difference and changed my life completely.

Even though I grew up in a loving and caring environment and always felt like I had a wonderful childhood, at the age of 27, when I first heard about affirmations, I was shocked that I could not affirm *"I like myself!"* and believe it.

At the age of 36, pregnant with my 3rd child, I remember standing at an Anthony Robbins seminar with 10,000 other people in London, crying my eyes out because I couldn't feel the love for the imaginary baby that represented myself.

Why was it easier for me to walk on hot burning coals just a day before than to believe that I deserved to be loved?

I found the answer a few years later when during a hypnosis session I discovered a cause of a distractive pattern of behavior and expectations that originated when I was an infant.

At a very young age, based on a dramatic event, I learned that people I love most cannot be trusted, that eventually I will get hurt and no one will protect me. For the next few decades, this core subconscious belief created havoc in my love life and helped cause some excruciatingly painful heartbreaking experiences.

Even though faces would change, history kept repeating itself, until I found the courage to get off the habitual treadmill and do something different by reaching out to others and getting some help.

Action Steps

- Most of us do not grow our own vegetables, make our own flower or cheese, or build our own houses. We do not build planes when we need to fly somewhere or build new computers when we need to use one. We hire accountants, lawyers, financial advisors, and see doctors when we are very sick. However, when it comes to sorting out our emotions and our lives, we often feel uncomfortable asking for help.
- Understand that you don't have to do this alone. There are people who dedicate their lives and years of education to help you create the kind of change that you want.
- The first time I gathered the courage to see a psychologist (and that was after being a life coach for over ten years), I remember walking out of her office feeling on Cloud Nine and thinking to myself, "Why?? Why didn't I do this before?!"
- If you need help, ask for it.

CHAPTER 9

ARE YOU AN EXPERT AT SURVIVING?

Getting off the treadmill of painful patterns, might seem like a logical thing to do, but it is scary. Those patterns are our comfort zone and we learn to live with them and to deal with them, to the point that we often don't even notice the discomfort and the pain anymore.

Consequently, many people become *experts at surviving, but not at finding true happiness.*

Too often, we fight to stay afloat, making ends meet, living day-to-day, month-by-month, and year-to-year, basically reliving the same patterns. And even though things get better at times and we can see a glimmer of hope, it is too often false or temporary hope. Without doing the work and making changes within ourselves, we will slip back into the same emotional rut, the same financial struggles, and the same relationship issues.

Things will not change unless we change!

I learned that the only way for us to shift our paradigm, the only way to finally break away from the familiar, unproductive comfort zone that allows us to do little more than survive, is to *create enough pain* so that the overwhelming fear of change and the unknown is a lot less scary.

Unfortunately, this is our human nature. Most people fear the unknown and change more than their present status, even if they are unhappy and their lives full of pain.

Why? Because out of the two driving forces that dictate all of our actions – Pain and Pleasure, pain is a much more powerful motivator.

The intelligent thing to do here, is to use this knowledge to our advantage and begin to manipulate ourselves to gather the courage to take the actions we were otherwise too afraid to take. Pain is like fire, we can make it work for us, instead of against us, if we learn its value.

Action Steps

- Think about a situation in your life that you would like to change. For example, do you feel frustrated with the lack of money to do what you want to do and when? Are you disappointed with someone in your life because they do not live up to your expectations? Are you unhappy with the way you look?
- Whatever it is that is causing you *emotional discomfort*, stop fighting it or pushing it away. Feel it fully. Feel what it would be like if the situation causing these emotions did not change for another five years. What about 10 years? What if over time, if left unattended and just pushed to the side, it got worse and worse?
- Experience the pain fully until it hurts so much you are willing to *shift your comfort zone* and to take action, because the fear of the unknown – of change – however painful that action might *seem*.
- Remind yourself that nothing and no one can hurt you without your permission and that you deserve better than that situation is offering you at the moment.

CHAPTER 10

WHAT DO YOU BELIEVE IN AND WHY?

"*We don't get what we want, we get what we believe.*" Kelley Rosano

Your beliefs greatly affect your reality and all your experiences. But how much control do you actually have over your beliefs?

For example, some people believe reincarnation exists and that there is such a thing as karma; others believe just as strongly that this is it – we are given this one life – we are born, make the most of it and die. Some believe strongly in heaven and in hell, others are happy to go through life believing in neither.

These examples are endless, from the origins of life and the universe, views on religion and spirituality, views on the best remedies for various ailments, on how best to raise children, the roles of men and women within a society and within a relationship or what might be the best way to make a carrot cake.

The curious question here is, how can someone believe strongly in one thing and someone else believe just as strongly in the completely opposite thing? Is one of them right and the other one wrong? Or maybe they are both wrong or both right? Are we somehow genetically predisposed to believe some things and not others?

Sandra Anne Taylor, author of the *New York Times* Bestseller, *Quantum Success: The astounding science of wealth and happiness*, observes that our belief system is a network of fundamental *assumptions* that we have *chosen* to embrace as a result of our upbringing and our personal experience.

So we CHOOSE what we believe in. Mostly subconsciously, but nevertheless, we choose our beliefs by *filtering* all that is happening to us and around us as part of our survival mechanism.

When we think about something long enough, charging those thoughts with focused emotions, we create beliefs, which then manifest themselves over and over in our lives supporting what we believe in, making us conclude that it must be the truth, where in fact, *it is an energetic creation or attraction of our own consistent thoughts and expectations.*

Action Steps

- What you believe in, you attract; what you believe in creates your reality as well as the emotions that you experience.
- When you are *tuned in to your emotions*, they act as a guiding system to show you which beliefs are consistent with who-you-are at your core and which ones are learned beliefs that go against your nature.
- When you let go of the beliefs that are holding you back and causing you to suffer, your life transforms and you eliminate a lot of unnecessary stress.
- At the same time, you can adopt new empowering beliefs which can make your life even more fabulous because your new beliefs will become your self-fulfilling prophesy.

CHAPTER 11

SELF-FULFILLING PROPHESY

One day my 9-year-old daughter came home from school and declared that she was not good in math and she could not be good in math because she heard someone say that girls are generally not good in math. Fortunately, by then I understood the power of self-fulfilling prophesy and the power of our beliefs, and I convinced her otherwise.

Even if my daughter was not born with extraordinary talents in math and science, (she is blessed with exceptional abilities in music, has an amazing voice and is a talented actress and dancer), by me helping her *believe* that she could excel in math too, she did! She worked hard and now, in her last year of high school, she has become one of the top students in her math class.

How many times have we been programmed to believe that based on our age, gender, heritage, nationality, zodiac sign or anything else outside of our true selves, we can or cannot excel in something? Can or cannot be a part of certain societies? Can or cannot have what we really desire?

Depending if we want to fit in or stand out, and which group of the society we want to be associated with, we either adopt or reject certain beliefs, creating our own points of references.

We then spend our lives judging events as right or wrong, positive or negative, wanted or unwanted, good or bad; not realizing that *we have the ability to control our personal relationship with all that happens to us, including how we react to it.*

However, *controlling* your thoughts and emotions does not mean BEING in control of them.

Controlling your thoughts or emotions by silencing them, pushing them away, and getting angry with yourself for having them, will only produce an outcome opposite to the one you desire.

Being in control of your thoughts and emotions is more about knowing how to guide them in the direction of your desires.

Action Steps

- Biologist Dr. Bruce H. Lipton in his popular best-selling book, *The Biology of Belief*, points out that, *"It is not gene-directed hormones and neurotransmitters that control our bodies and our minds; our beliefs control our bodies and minds, and thus our lives."*
- So, if your beliefs control your life and you are in charge of creating them, what can you do to make this creating of beliefs a conscious process and use them as tools in building your life masterpiece?
- *Consciously creating the story of your reality* requires:
    - Giving attention to how you feel, and
    - Being connected and congruent emotionally, mentally, and physically.

In the next three chapters we will examine each of these elements separately and learn how to work with all of them to create the best reality possible.

CHAPTER 12

YOUR PHYSICAL BODY

Your body is a phenomenal tool for helping guide you to your true desires and to the purpose of your higher self. Your body is always 'talking' to you through physical pains and discomforts, pointing out where your attention should be given.

Bodily pain and discomfort is an indication that there is either an energetic block (too much energy is concentrated in one place) or not enough energy is flowing into that particular area. At the same time, and I find this fascinating, each part of your body is connected to a particular emotion!

For example, a headache indicates self-criticism and being unhappy with yourself and your actions. Pain in your back indicates a lack of emotional support. Depending on what part of your back is painful, it could mean worry about financial support (in the lower region), feelings of guilt (towards the middle), or feeling too much responsibility (shoulders and upper back).

There are metaphysical and psychological reasons for allergies, for having a fever, for breaking or hurting a particular finger, for losing hair, for hip or knee pain, for twisting an ankle, getting an infection, and so on. Most people point out to outside causes of being sick, but my research and personal experience have lead me to conclude that most of our pain is internally created and driven.

Action Steps

- If something is causing you physical discomfort, do not rush to numb the pain with drugs. If you don't locate and deal with the emotional and internal causes, the pain will most likely resurface again at a later time or lead to other problems.
- You can refer to the chart in the Appendix II of this book to find out what might have triggered this pain on an emotional level.
- Even in cases when you have to see a doctor and take medication, try to understand the underlying psychological cause of the pain to prevent it from becoming chronic.

CHAPTER 13

YOUR EMOTIONAL BODY

Emotions are your best friends when it comes to being a *conscious creator* of your life masterpiece. They create your reality by indicating what you are currently *attracting* into your reality based on what you are feeling.

Rather than labeling our emotions with words like anger, disappointment, love, appreciation, or sadness, let's divide all our emotions into two basic categories, pleasant or feel-good emotions, and unpleasant or feel-bad emotions.

Unpleasant and painful emotions are created when we focus on what we don't have; when we experience unmet expectations; and most of all, when we feel fear.

On the other hand, when we feel wonderful and experience all kinds of feel-good emotions, we are tuned in to the frequency of the energetic vibration of wellbeing and of our desires where our thoughts and actions are in alignment with that.

Though our emotions are our friends and teachers, they don't *own* us and should not become a part of us. Therefore, pay attention to how you speak. For example, instead of saying "I *am* angry," it is better to say "I *feel* angry," instead of saying "I *am* sad," say "I *feel* sad."

This is because you *are not* anger or sadness, you are *experiencing* anger or sadness; the emotion is 'visiting' you temporarily to teach you something. Feel it, welcome it, ask what you can learn from it and then let it go or transform it into a different, more pleasant emotion.

When we consciously separate ourselves from our emotions, it makes it possible for us to release them. Emotions are not meant to get stuck, as they often do, inside of us. They come to teach us and then they are meant to go.

Action Steps

- To release unwanted emotions please refer to the Appendix I or Appendix II at the end of this book.

CHAPTER 14

YOUR MENTAL BODY

Your mind is the third integral ingredient to the equation of the holistic approach of your Being and the creation of your life. It is responsible for the *thoughts*, which in turn create corresponding *emotions*, which in turn make your *body* respond with either pain or vitality and well-being.

Have you ever stopped and wondered about the process of thinking? Simply put, *thinking is a process where you ask yourself a question and then answer it to yourself.*

When we are trying to think ourselves out of a situation, we often don't find an appropriate solution because we are limited to what we already know and have already experienced, which is often not enough. As Albert Einstein concluded:

"*We cannot solve our problems with the same thinking we used when we created them.*"

Thinking used to be one of my favorite pastimes. I loved to think. I could do it for hours; in fact, I believe I rarely stopped thinking and I thought that all people did that until someone pointed out that it was not the case. I also used to think that thinking all the time was something admirable until I started yoga and meditation.

Over time, though, I learned that thinking all the time can be a dangerous process and something we need to do sparingly because it can lead you on a downward spiral and take over you, causing you to experience negative emotions that otherwise would not be there.

When I learned to let go of my habit of constantly staying in my conscious, thinking mind, I became calmer, more confident and centered, as well as wiser and less reactive. I still like to think, but now I am a lot more aware and in control of my thoughts and I guide them rather than being guided by them.

Action Steps

- To find a creative solution to a problem, it is important to get outside of our existing knowledge and experience and either ask for help or go within and meditate.
- You can ask for help to get a different perspective; to look at a situation from another point of view.
- Through meditation, you can access the knowledge of your higher self and connect to the Universal Mind – the energy field that connects us all.
- By meditating you also disconnect yourself from the problem and become an observer, removing the *emotional charge* from it and, therefore, being in a much better position to find the right solution.

PART 2

EMOTIONS THAT CAUSE US PAIN AND SUFFERING

CHAPTER 15

WHY DO WE SUFFER?

Why do we suffer physical and emotional pain, sometimes to the point where the pain is unbearable? In those times of despair and pain, life seems to lose all meaning and all we want is for the pain to end, while we feel that it will probably go on forever. Most of us have suffered that kind of pain in our lives and it can make us feel alone and left wondering why we were chosen to undergo such a seemingly useless ordeal.

Yet, such ordeals are not useless. I refuse to believe that we are given anything in our life without a good reason, even pain and suffering. If we learn to understand it and work with it, it can become our guide and not the enemy.

Let me ask you what seems like a very random question – *do you know how lobsters grow?*

A lobster is a soft mushy animal that lives inside an inflexible shell. The shell is too rigid to stretch and expand and yet, the lobster keeps growing. How?

The mushy lobster inside grows and becomes very uncomfortable and confined inside a small shell to the point that it needs to find a safe place and shed or get rid of the old, small, and useless shell and then it produces another one that fits it perfectly.

As time passes, the lobster inside the new shell is still growing but the shell stays the same, so the uncomfortable lobster sheds the shell that is causing pain and produces a new one. This process repeats itself until lobster reaches its full size.

So the only way for the lobster to be able to grow, is to feel uncomfortable and to change its environment to suit his new size.

But, what if a lobster could go and see a doctor who prescribed medication to numb the pain and the uncomfortable feeling? I assume the lobster would just die in the small shell, possibly pain-free but never reaching its full potential.

Action Steps

- Pain is uncomfortable, to say the least, but it is there for a reason. It is there to indicate to us that we have outgrown the old patterns of living and reacting (our old shell) and that a *shift or a change is necessary for us to continue on our journey of life.*
- Pain is caused by resistance. *Resistance to who we really are* and a false projection of a "reality" that doesn't match our true being.
- If you have suffered, have felt uncomfortable, with some of the emotions described in this section and you feel ready to shed them as the lobster does with his shell, then realize that the new approach is needed. Stay open-minded and follow the suggested action steps.
- But before you do that, decide that you have suffered enough, you have struggled enough, and you have sacrificed enough. You deserve to be pain free.

CHAPTER 16

THE PAIN OF FEAR AND RESISTANCE

Most of the suffering we experience has its roots in fear and fear is a result of self-dissatisfaction with who we are and what we have; it also has to do with not feeling enough or not having enough.

In fact, every negative emotion we experience stems from a certain fears we have. When you feel anger, you are fearful of something. When you worry, when you get frustrated, when you get disappointed, when you feel sad – it is basically an expression of fear at some level.

For example, you might get angry at your child for not being a good student or for not cleaning her room. The underlying fear here might be that you raised a child who is not as smart or as tidy or as respectful as you want him or her to be; you fear that you haven't been a good parent and that you might have failed somehow. Your sense of identity gets threatened.

Worry, for example, is a fear that something will not go as you want it to, and you fear possible pain of the outcome of that.

When we feel sad or when we grieve for something, we fear that we might never have what we had, ever again, and that we might never be happy again.

We fear disappointing people we care about; we fear not being enough for them; not being enough in our own eyes; not doing enough, not having enough. The list goes on.

Living in fear is painful and slows down your progress. It poisons your life but it also points out the direction where you need to *let go and release the grip* – let go of control and just trust. Trust and have faith.

Faith gives you freedom to live. Fear robs you of that freedom.

The Pain of Fear and Resistance | **35**

Action Steps

- If you are asked what fear feels like, can you describe the feeling? Is it that familiar uneasy, uncomfortable feeling in your gut? Is it the kind of feeling that shuts down your thinking ability or is so strong that it makes you feel debilitated physically as well?
- I am asking you these questions because most of the time we feel something, but are not sure why and therefore, cannot adequately react and deal with that emotion.
- When you understand what fear feels like for you, then you know that at this moment you are feeling fear and it's ok.
- Ask yourself, what was it that triggered the fear? Often our reaction to fear is automatic and pre-programed from years ago. When we understand what is truly causing the fear, it is much easier to let it go.

CHAPTER 17

MY CAVING ADVENTURE AND WHAT IT TAUGHT ME

I decided some time ago that *I will do the things that I fear* and release myself from its grip and control. One example of facing my fears was my caving adventure! Let me share it with you…

Some people are very sporty and fit, some people love extreme sports and don't mind getting dirty in the process. Well, that is not me. I don't even like to go to the beach because there is sand and it gets into places and I was never sporty and doing anything like that is way out of my comfort zone.

However, when one of my clients, a world champion in wrestling, shared with me that he was opening a new company that offered extreme sports adventures to people, and then asked me if I would explore one of the adventures with him and his team before he offered it the public, I agreed. First, because I support my clients and friends, and second, because I had no idea what I was getting myself into.

So, a couple of days later, my very fit client, his three team members – all professional sportsmen, me, and another friend of mine I asked to join us, because I didn't want to be the only female and she also happened to be a fitness instructor and a former Olympic champion, put on our robes and gears and faced the cave.

I must add that by then I already had three children, with the youngest being only two years old and I was honestly tired by the time I climbed a little hill to get to the entrance of the cave! Of course I didn't share it with my team as I never liked being the weak one.

The cave was deserted and someone in the group stopped to ask if anyone in the outside world knew where we were. Apparently, the guide's mother did and that seemed sufficient. Naturally, I didn't tell my mother about it until after it happened just in case she decided to talk me out of it.

We went into the dark cave and started climbing the inside wall laughing and feeling excited. Not too bad, I thought to myself, until we arrived to the edge of a 25-meter drop!

I was the only one who had never gone abseiling before. Now I was just *pretending* to laugh and to be excited. Everyone reassured me and said that as long as I leaned back far enough (perpendicular to the wall) I should not crash into the wall, which is the worst that can happen, they said, adding… well, except for the rope snapping and you falling down, but that is very unlikely!

I've lived to say that I made it down without hitting the wall, though slower than everyone else. But, all the cheers and high-fives made me feel good and with renewed confidence we proceeded to the Room of Death.

The Room of Death was given its name because it has a natural stone formation very closely resembling a skeleton AND it is filled with bats! Hundreds of them! When I asked what the strange soft soil that we were walking on and the slime on the walls we had to hold on to was, I was told that it was the bat droppings! Yuck! Again, I just pretended to be excited…

With no lights in the cave and just our little lights on the helmets to illuminate the next few steps ahead, it was spooky, not to mention dangerous drops everywhere and super slippery stones that we had to climb up and down. Not surprisingly, my shoes were very wrong for it!

Besides slipping once and falling on my face (fortunately not into the bat poo), I was doing very well until we crawled into a small enclave that had a tiny hole (and I mean tiny!), leading G-d knows where and the guide told me to proceed, which could only be done lying down on my back and wiggling myself through a tight cavity in the earth. Suddenly I felt claustrophobic and my fear of being stuck in a small tight place paralyzed me and I said, "I am not going down that hole!"

Eventually, most of the group had successfully crawled through the trench, though with some grunts and complaints of dirt falling into their mouths. There was no going back and I had no choice but to face my fear of claustrophobia, so I got on my back and tried not to think of the tube of dirty walls surrounding me 360° and pretended to be a worm wiggling my way down.

With encouragements and cheers I made it down, and once again felt really good about myself and about overcoming my fear!

Two hours later we reached the final climb, which was small, but the most dangerous. Unfortunately, I looked down and saw the drop and looked at my slippery shoes and that no one was there to support me. I froze once again and yelled for the guide to help me but he was too far ahead and couldn't turn around in the narrow passage. He said calmly, *"You can do it,"* and stayed where he was.

And I did it! I pulled myself up using the muscles I didn't know I had, crossed the narrow passage over the sheer drop in my wrong slippery shoes, I slid down the seven meters on the stone and I was out!

With high-fives and high-tens, jumps and hugs, feeling at the same time a little stupid and crazy for putting ourselves through this, but also proud and more confident about ourselves and our abilities, we completed our Caving Adventure!

Did I feel fear? Yes! More than once and more than once I wanted to turn around and go back. But, like most times in life, there is no turning back and the only way is forward, whether we like it or not, whether we are scared or not, done it before or not, fit and experienced or not.

The truth is, during that experience I proved to myself once again that all I need in order to get to the other side is knowing where to put my hand and my foot next (having goals and a vision); having enough light (knowledge and wisdom) to see that next opening; staying focused (live in the moment); and the importance of surrounding myself with capable, supportive, and fun people to make my journey in life faster and more enjoyable!

Yes, fear is a powerful emotion capable of keeping us within the confines of our comfort zones, stagnating our growth and progress and basically controlling our lives.

BUT, you are more powerful!

Action Steps

- You can train yourself to do the things that you fear, even if just to prove to yourself that you are capable of doing what you think you cannot.
- The good news is, the more you do it, the easier it gets. It is like *training your fearless muscle*. You become more confident, stronger, wiser, as well as more compassionate and understanding of others and what they are going through.
- So *make a decision to do the things you fear and to train YOUR fearless muscle.*
- Think of something that you fear and have always avoided. It can be a difficult conversation with someone, or something adventurous like sky-diving. The first thing that comes to mind, make a decision to do it and follow through! When you come out on the other side, you will be a different, more confident and happier person!

P.S. Please remember that it is important to differentiate between the fear that is holding back your progress and the fear that is warning you not to do something stupid that will take you in the opposite direction of what is best for your progress. *Always stay aware of the consequences of your decisions.*

CHAPTER 18

THE PAIN OF GRIEF AND DESPAIR

When it comes to emotions, grief and despair have some of the lowest vibrational frequencies. And yet, it is difficult to go through life without experiencing these very painful emotions. Usually these emotions are associated with the feeling of loss – loss of the loved one, loss of a relationship, loss of material possessions that meant a lot to us, loss of hope.

Often, we get impatient with these emotions and want to push them away and run away from them, or camouflage or deny they exist, not giving ourselves enough time to just feel and just be, and, therefore, to heal.

Many books are written on the stages of grieving. Allow yourself to go through those stages and to experience them, reminding yourself that it will pass and you will be happy again.

Action Steps

- Although most people at this stage want to be alone and hide from the world, it is best to reach out to people you trust and/or get professional help. Otherwise, alone with your thoughts, you are risking a downward spiral.

CHAPTER 19

THE PAIN OF MISSING SOMEONE

Being separated from someone you love or really like, whether temporary or due to a break-up, creates a void that can be very painful. The stronger the chemical imbalance created by the separation, the stronger you would feel the pain of that void, which is actually the kind of withdrawal symptoms people experience when they crave drugs, alcohol, smoking, or any others addiction.

The intensity of the pain is also the strongest during the initial stages of separation, while the body is readjusting itself to the lack of the chemicals.

During the withdrawal stages of missing someone we often make irrational decisions and behave in a way that can surprise us, feeling clingy, dependent, and lost.

But the truth is, you are whole and complete without the person that you are so desperately missing and want to reconnect with; though this knowledge gets clouded or disappears completely from our conscious when we lose the connection with our inner self and in desperation to feel "normal" again, make a mistake to achieve it externally.

If we can't be with that person whom we believe can make us feel better, we often rush to find someone else to fill the hole or numb our pain by alcohol, drugs, or other distractive behavior. This creates a downward spiral and further disconnects us from becoming whole, independent and finding our true power.

What to do?

Action Steps

- First, allow yourself to miss the other person. Realize that if you miss someone, it is because you felt very good together and be grateful for the gifts of that union while it lasted. We also often grieve over the possibility of what might-have-been.
- Understand that if you could experience it once with someone, you have the capacity to experience it again. Everything is your creation. Just write a new script, taking into consideration the lessons you learned, and trust that the next time it will be even better!
- Finally, give yourself and your body time to re-adjust. Be kind to yourself. Don't judge or get angry and disappointed with yourself. Allow yourself to feel.
- The more you fight what you feel, the longer it will stay. When you *just let it be*, without judgment and impatience, you will recover much faster and will build your self-esteem and self-confidence in the process.

CHAPTER 20

THE PAIN OF FEELING GUILT AND SHAME

Unfortunately, we often suffer because we feel we deserve to suffer. We allow others to hurt us because subconsciously we want to be hurt, want to be punished, and we expect it from others.

These emotions are usually guided by a misplaced feelings of guilt and shame.

But what is guilt? According to Deepak Chopra, *"Guilt is a perception, and all perceptions are open to change."*

This is a powerful statement. Everything that we feel in life and everything that we experience is a perception based on our own interpretation of events, our values, and our dependency to fit into the society we live in.

I often remind myself, especially at times when things are hard or I feel scared about something, that I am experiencing a perception, *an illusion of my own creation* and if I don't like what is happening to me right now, I can just change it and create a different illusion.

If guilt is a self-imposed emotion and emotions are not who we are, it is reasonable then to conclude that we can let go of that emotion any time we *choose* to. The trouble is, most people desperately like to hold on to the emotion of guilt because somehow they feel it justifies what they have done.

But, who actually benefits if you are feeling guilty? No one of course. And whose health gets ruined and whose progress is stunted because of you feeling guilty? Yours of course.

There is really no benefit to this extremely distractive emotion. And these are not just empty words. Guilt, and even more so, shame, are the most self-destructive emotions that slowly, but surely, destroy us in the sneakiest of ways without us realizing what is happening.

Action Steps

- If you did something that awakens the emotions of guilt, admit it, take responsibility for what you did, do what you can to fix it and choose to feel good about yourself in the process.
- Ask for forgiveness of the person you might have hurt and always ask yourself for forgiveness too.
- Forgive yourself and let it go. If the other person wants to hold on to resentment, it is up to them to work through it.
- Learn from your mistakes, but do not hold on to them by allowing guilt to take over you and control you.

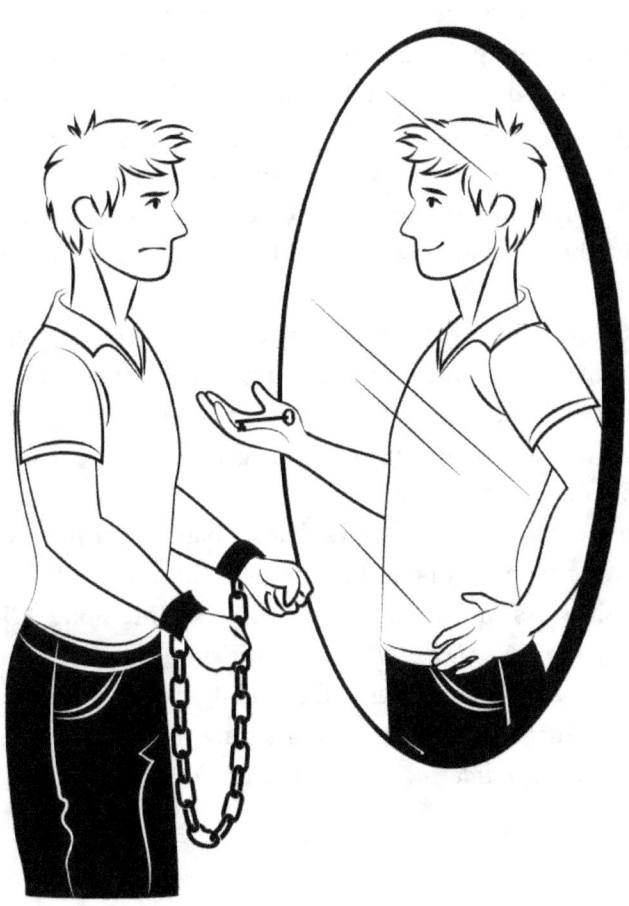

CHAPTER 21

THE PAIN OF RESENTMENT AND HOW TO FORGIVE

Resentment and lack of forgiveness take away our power, or more accurately, we give away that power to someone else. We become permanently connected to the person whom we refuse to forgive until we are ready to let it go.

People often say, *"This is not forgivable,"* or *"I cannot forgive,"* and yet, forgiving, as much as holding on to resentment, is a choice, although it isn't often an easy one.

Sometimes we make the mistake of holding on to the blame and resentment, believing we are punishing the person who caused us pain and it also makes us feel righteous. As Mike Dooly, best-selling author and one of the featured expert in *The Secret* says, *"The best way to forgive is not to blame."*

In fact, the only way to forgive is to stop blaming, stop judging and stop acting out the programming meant to keep us in fear – the fear that it might happen again, the fear that we will get hurt again, the fear that we are not good enough.

Complete forgiveness happens when you 'get it'. It is not really a step-by-step mental process of doing this and doing that and then, presto! All is forgotten and forgiven. It might work temporarily, but more often than not, it shows its ugly face again; possibly camouflaged in a different scenario played out with the same or different people.

Taking responsibility for the roles that we play in our life dramas and, in fact, for creating them, is one of the hardest things to do. But, hard doesn't mean impossible. As Mahatma Gandhi wisely pointed out, *"The weak can never forgive. Forgiveness is the attribute of the strong."*

In this case, being strong doesn't mean that you have to force forgiveness out of yourself; that never works. Being strong means completely *accepting* the situation as is, *surrendering* to it, to its pain, to its lessons, and to the energetic power of it.

Action Steps

- Surrender yourself to *the experience* and make a decision not to participate in this particular drama any more.
- Allow yourself the freedom from resentment, judgement, and blame. You deserve it!

CHAPTER 22

THE PAIN OF NOT FEELING IN CONTROL

It is reasonable to say that no one and nothing belongs to us and everyone and everything has the right to exist without us.

However, it is human nature to want to control people and circumstances that we feel are causing or might be causing us pain. The more we try to control, though, the more pain and fear we feel because our subconscious knows that control is illusionary and temporary and that pain always returns unless you see it for what it is, accept it and remove the importance of it.

People who try to be in control all the time are a lot more stressed, unhappy, and disappointed on a regular basis than those who have learned to let go of control and allow things to happen and to fall into place.

Just to clarify, when I talk about control, I refer to wanting to control people and circumstances. You can and should have control of the direction of your thoughts and your focus as well as control of your emotional reactions or outbursts that are based in anger and fear.

Action Steps

- You can learn to release the grip of control and eventually let it go completely by doing regular meditations and developing an inner sense of trust and faith.
- Your life should not be forced and controlled; it should be allowed to flow naturally with *clarity of the general direction,* and with *the power of confidence and faith.*

CHAPTER 23

THE PAIN OF FAILURE

Successful people see failure as a stepping stone to success rather than something to get depressed about. For example, Thomas Watson, founder of IBM, believed that *"In order to succeed you need to double your failure rate."*

George Bernard Shaw, famous Irish playwright and critic, said, "*I observed that nine out of ten things I did were failures. I didn't want to be a failure so I did ten times more work.*"

According to these and other highly successful individuals, the more you fail, the more successful you become; or the more you see failure as *an essential part of the success process*, the more likely you would have the courage and self-discipline to get to the final line.

It is important to understand that the pain of failure is experienced not based on failing to do something, but based on our initial expectations of ourselves and our own interpretation of the events.

Finally, if, no matter what happens to you, you get up, dust yourself off and try again, armed with the new knowledge and experience, then you have a healthy attitude to what some might consider failure. It means that you do understand that it is not falling down but staying down that keeps us from progress and stuck in our comfort zone and in our fear.

Action Steps

To prevent yourself from feeling the pain of failure:

- Re-examine your expectations;
- Control your inner chatter and your interpretation of the events;
- Develop a healthy attitude to failure, if you have not done that already, and be an example to others by bouncing higher than you fall.

CHAPTER 24

THE PAIN OF FEELING INSIGNIFICANT, UNIMPORTANT, AND NOT NEEDED

It is easy to feel insignificant if we ponder the vastness and the magnificence of this universe. Even if we just focus on our planet, being one in the mass of billions, fulfilling our desire for significance and individuality seems daunting. And yet, feeling significant and knowing that we are valued is one of the basic human needs that drive many of our life's choices.

When I first became an immigrant to the United States of America, I was just 17 years-old and I remember thinking to myself, how can this little Russian girl, with no language, no money, no contacts and a very different mindset, do something to get noticed? To feel valued and significant? To change the world?

Then I read an article about a research meteorologist at the Massachusetts Institute of Technology, Edward Lorenz, who in 1961, concluded that the movements of a butterfly's wings in San Francisco can affect the weather in Shanghai! The formal name for this phenomenon is *"sensitive dependence on initial conditions,"* and the more popular name is the *Butterfly Effect*.

If a little butterfly has such power, how powerful then are we?

I learned that every thought that I think, every action that I take or don't take, even my intentions carry enormous power and affect this world.

And I decided that I can and I will change the world by first changing myself – by becoming the best I can be, the happiest I can be, living my life to the fullest and being proud of myself.

What if all of us made that goal and found happiness, contentment, and fulfilment in the process? Then this world would be filled with happy, content, and fulfilled individuals who respect, accept, and love themselves; and therefore, they respect, accept, and love everyone around them. Hence, there would be no need for wars, conflict and domination since nobody would feel insecure and feel the need to gain their significance by controlling, destroying, and manipulating others.

Action Steps

- If everyone took full responsibility for their own happiness, guided by love and acceptance, achieving the changes we would like to see in this world would be a lot more possible.
- Taking back your power to be the creator of your own life is the best thing you can do to make this world a happier and better place and to set an example for others to do the same.

CHAPTER 25

THE PAIN OF ANGER AND RESENTMENT

Anger, whether contained or expressed, is an emotion that is based in fear and often camouflages other painful emotions such as guilt, feelings of unworthiness, fear of being wrong or incapable, the pain of being criticized or belittled or the feeling of being misunderstood.

When anger is left unattended, it leads to resentment. Tiffany Watt Smith, author of the *Book of Human Emotions*, describes resentment as, *"The hatred we suppress when forbidden to give voice to the ways we are hurt or humiliated or frustrated, a wound caused by our own dependency."*

As human beings, we all experience anger in one form or another. Suppressing anger, as well as other destructive emotions, of course, is very unhealthy, though giving yourself time to cool off and understand the emotions that lead you to feel angry is important.

Emotions of anger surface when we are being out of alignment with who we really are, when we behave in an incongruent way with our true self – *and when the masks that we put on ourselves in order to survive are being challenged.*

Resentment often becomes a part of our story, which we hold on to because it gives us significance and validates our victim mentality.

When you get tired of being a victim and are ready to rewrite your story, you will let go of resentment as you will feel no more need to hold on to this very damaging emotion.

The Pain of Anger and Resentment | **55**

> **Action Steps**
> - The next time you experience a flare of anger, do not get disappointed with yourself; rather feel grateful and try a different approach.
> - Take the blame away from the person or a situation that is causing you anger.
> - Think about the underlying emotion causing the anger and the ways in which it is challenging you.
> - Accept that about yourself, make changes if necessary, and feel grateful.

Most of us get angry about the same few unattended, underlying emotions which, when understood, disappear, taking with them our reactions of anger and resentment.

CHAPTER 26

THE PAIN OF JEALOUSY IN A RELATIONSHIP

Jealousy is a complicated emotion. Some people falsely believe that it is an integral part of love, that if you love someone, it is inevitable to feel jealous. They believe if someone doesn't feel jealousy they don't really love the other person. This, of course, is another example of a false conditioning of many societies which leads to unneeded suffering and many break-ups.

Jealousy, in fact, is an emotion of insecurity and possessiveness. A jealous person believes that the one they love is theirs and only theirs, and when the suspicion of a rival, even if this suspicion is imaginary, arises, so does the jealousy.

The insecurity arises from the feeling that we are not good enough and someone better will eventually come and take away what we want, take away the one we love; or the one we love will inevitably find someone better and more suitable. In this scenario, the person who is jealous is seen as a victim, the one they love as a traitor, and the one they lose their loved one to as a thief. The painful experience is further deepened by the pain of feeling humiliated, discarded, and replaced.

An insecure person then becomes even more insecure, with their feelings of self-esteem and self-worth crashing to the ground and their victim mentality reinforced, followed by more experiences that deepen these emotions.

A wise person would not have the desire to possess and would understand that we don't belong to anyone and that no one belongs to us. Trying to control someone or allowing someone to control you is not love, it is dependency and insecurity.

A loving relationship is based on trust and if the person we love has been dishonest, we have choices to react in a much healthier way than jealousy. By making those choices, we reinforce our love and respect for who we are and strengthen our confidence rather than destroy it.

Action Steps

- If you mistrust someone without a reason, examine your own honesty. Do you feel you can be trusted? People who feel they cannot be trusted are always suspicious and jealous of others.
- If you are fearful or expect someone to cheat or to leave you, chances are – they will. What we fear we attract.
- If you suspect someone has been dishonest, do not question, probe and nag, just tell them that you trust them and that you love them. This kind of attitude can save a relationship, if it is a one-off mistake.
- If you know that the other person is dishonest on a regular basis, then show yourself respect and know that there is someone, in fact there are many people, who will also show you respect by being honest and loving.
- Finally, never be afraid to lose what you have. Trust that no matter what happens, you will always be loved, protected, and complete.

"If you love a flower, don't pick it up. Because if you pick it up it dies and it ceases to be what you love. So if you love a flower, let it be. Love is not about possession. Love is about appreciation." Osho

CHAPTER 27

THE PAIN OF DOUBT AND WORRY

Worry is an uneasy feeling that something might or has gone wrong, that something will not live up to your expectations and that, as a consequence, it will be an unpleasant or painful experience.

Have you ever stopped and thought about what the process of worrying really is?

When we worry, we visualize or imagine an unwanted outcome and then become stressed about it. This is not just unnecessary stress, this is also a dangerous process since what we focus on, we attract.

I am not here to tell you not to worry. For most people, that is not possible. The good news is that you can learn to use worry to your advantage. The next time you find yourself visualizing an unwanted outcome, stop and think about the ideal scenario in this situation and send your energy in that direction.

Action Steps

- If you worry about an upcoming job interview or an important business meeting, you can visualize how easily the conversation flows, how confident and relaxed you are feeling throughout the whole meeting and how you shake hands in agreement.
- If you worry about not having enough money at the end of the month, channel your focus on all the things that you do have, feel gratitude for all that you are able to afford and get into that space of abundance rather than lack.
- If you worry about the safety of your loved one, imagine how you are enjoying each other's company in a near future safe and sound.
- Take any situation that you worry about and move your focus from that space of lack or fear, into a space of trust and abundance.

CHAPTER 28

THE PAIN OF ANXIETY

Anxiety is basically an extreme case of worry taken to a level that makes you physically unhealthy. The frustrating part about anxiety is knowing that there is no reason to be freaked out, but at the same time, feeling helpless to stop those negative emotions from taking over.

However, *feeling* helpless when the anxiety takes over does not mean that you actually are helpless, you just don't have the tools yet to help you deal with the flow of emotions adequately.

Anxiety is an emotion that belongs in the future, therefore, one way to control it is to focus on the present moment and get grounded. As soon as you feel an anxious feeling coming on, look around and notice five things you can see, four things you can touch, three things you can hear, two things you can smell, and one things you can taste. This will bring your attention to here-and-now and will take your mind off the addictive thought pattern that sucks you in and makes you feel out of control and fearful.

Anxiety also happens when you think you need to figure out everything at once. There is an underlying reason for everything that we do and everything that we get to experience and this underlying reason serves your ego. Ego likes to be busy because the busier we are, the more phone calls and emails we get, the more people there are who rely on us, the more valuable, needed and important we feel.

You don't need to overwhelm yourself with things to do to feel worthy of achieving your goals and of being loved, valued, and accepted.

One thing I realized is that the more I do, the more there is to do. At the same time, I've learned that the more time I take to get grounded and centered, and the more time I take to relax and reflect, the happier I feel and the more productive I get. This, in turn, also helps me attract situation, circumstances, and people who help me reach my goals faster and easier, without the stress and anxiety.

The Pain of Anxiety | 61

Action Steps

- Most of us, of course, at some point in our lives, do experience emotions of anxiety, and some people feel anxious much of their lives. If you are one of them, do not let it bring you down or make you feel inadequate or not good enough. Remind yourself that you have what it takes to deal with any situation, you just haven't figured out how yet.
- Do not try to do it all by yourself. Reach out to people who can help with whatever makes you anxious and with the emotion of anxiety as well.
- Nothing in this life is more important than you and your well-being. Make yourself and your health a priority and schedule yoga, meditation, dance, art, or sports activates – anything that helps you get grounded, relaxes your mind and feeds your soul.
- Finally, use this mantra when the feeling of anxiety comes over: *"I am exactly where I need to me, doing exactly what I need to be doing, and it is an absolute perfection!"*

CHAPTER 29

THE PAIN OF FEELING OVERWHELMED AND DISCOURAGED

In an attempt to keep up with the high speed of today's life, and with the 'ideal' life-style, or a 'perfect' wife, mother, husband, entrepreneur, etc., portrayed by many societies, we often experience the emotion of being overwhelmed and, as a consequence, discouraged.

Sometimes a mere idea of something can be overwhelming and we give up before even starting.

When I got unexpectedly pregnant with a third child, I was already very busy with a three-year old and a seven-year-old, my career was booming and I just decided to publish a book. I thought to myself, *"How can I possibly run a business, look after two young children, run a household, and publish a book while pregnant?"*

At first, the thought overwhelmed me, but quickly I made a decision to take it one day, one task at a time. Just one phone call, I would tell myself, one email, one follow-up, one coaching session, one dinner, one night-time story, one page of the book, and so on.

Eight months later I felt like I gave birth to two babies – my son and my book. It was one of the happiest moments of my life as a photo was taken of me holding my new-born baby in one hand and my new-born book in the other.

The Pain of Feeling Overwhelmed and Discouraged | **63**

> **Action Steps**
>
> - Your brain can handle different topics over a period of time, but it can only focus on one thing at a time, and when presented with too many tasks at once, it can shut down or not do those tasks effectively.
> - When life and its demands overwhelm you, break it all down into chewable, manageable, small tasks and focus on those little tasks only.
> - Before you know it, one step at a time, one task at a time, it will all get done.

CHAPTER 30

THE PAIN OF DISAPPOINTMENT

We get disappointed when our expectations are not being realized, when we feel deprived of what was 'rightfully' ours and feel disposed and pushed to the side, when hopes are crushed and our hearts fill with sadness and at times, bewilderment.

Although experiencing disappointment is unpleasant, it serves as a wake-up call to adjust what is often unrealistic, often ego-driven expectations, defined by Sigmund Freud as "narcissistic wounds." In this case, our sense of identity is being threatened and the fear of not living up to or being who we *imagined* ourselves to be causes us pain and suffering.

Another reason for feeling disappointment is when the stories we create for ourselves do not materialize as we imagine them – the knights in white and shining armor, the happily-ever-after relationships, and the joy that doesn't last once some goals are finally achieved.

There are many stories of Olympic champions who experience a down instead of an elation when after excruciatingly hard work they finally achieve their life-long dream.

I have experienced this kind of disappointment the day after my book, *The One Minute Coach: Change your life one minute at a time*, became a best-seller. There is an added emotion of being disappointed with yourself for even feeling disappointed because you feel foolish, but the overwhelming emotion of, "Now what?" takes over and for a while, life seems to lose its meaning and purpose.

Action Steps

To avoid the empty and confusing feeling of disappointment, it is important to:

- Focus on the process and not the end result – *enjoy the process* to the fullest rather than waiting for happiness when your goal is reached.
- Don't look at a disappointing experience as a failure. Instead, look at it as a correction of unrealistic stories or expectations.

CHAPTER 31

THE PAIN OF FEELING FRUSTRATED, IRRITATED, AND IMPATIENT

'Practice makes perfect', as the saying goes. Although we usually hear it as a motivation to excel in some skill, this saying applies to *everything* that we do in life.

If you get angry often enough, it becomes your habitual reaction. If you get frustrated or irritated over and over, it becomes your habitual reaction. It is the same with impatience and any other negative outbursts. We often perfect the skill of being negative, at times by observing those close to us, and reacting in a way that trains us to experience it again and again.

When we feel frustrated, irritated, and impatient, we basically feel that we are losing control of someone or of a situation. We also feel that the person or the situation is not living up to our expectations.

The true meaning of being out of control is when you give away your power to a person or a situation that you find frustrating or irritating.

We also often feel frustrated with *ourselves* because we do not live up to our own expectations or do not fit into the idea of who we are and how we should behave – *when the blueprint of what our lives should be like and the role that we should be playing in it is out of sync.*

But however unpleasant frustration feels, as with all emotions, it is here to make things better, to guide you in the direction of your higher purpose. So if you are feeling stuck or feeling that something you are waiting for will never happen, this emotion is a powerful indicator that a change is needed.

Action Steps

- Be careful not to turn negative reactions into a habit. Observe how and when you react and when needed, *break the pattern* by doing something completely different.
- When frustration comes up, think about what new paths it is trying to show you or what old paths it is time to turn away from. Let go of the fear of change and let frustration be the bridge that can connect you to where you really need to be.

CHAPTER 32

THE PAIN OF BOREDOM

Surprisingly, one of the emotions that most people want to avoid is boredom – an emotion that makes us feel unmotivated, disinterested, weak, fed up, with a vague sense that you want something to change but have no idea what.

When we feel bored, we feel stagnant. We feel useless and, therefore, inadequate. Boredom often leads to unhealthy behavior such as excessive drinking or drug use, excessive sleeping and eating.

No wonder people try to avoid boredom like a plague and fill their days, as well as the days of their children, with endless activities.

However, according to Tiffany Watt Smith, the author of the *Book of Human Emotions*, slipping into boredom *"gives rise to pleasant reverie and daydreams,"* which then leads to being inventive and imaginary and puts people in a creative state.

Action Steps

- Next time you find yourself feeling bored, don't get scared and don't rush to change it. Allow yourself to sit with that emotion and see what creative ideas and solutions might come to you.
- Do not rush to fill your child's timetable with too many activities. Children need to learn how to entertain themselves without relying on other people, TV programs, or electronic games to do it for them. Allow your kids to use their creativity before they will become too dependent on the outside stimuli.

CHAPTER 33

AVOIDING DISAPPOINTMENTS AND ARGUMENTS

Imagine two people, each with their own interpretation of the same event, and with interpretations that match their own stories rather than describing what has really happened – each person trying hard to support their view and to prove their truth just to be confronted with an equal determination of the other person trying to do the same.

The analogy I like to use here is of four people who looked at the same house, but from four different sides and those sides only.

Let's imagine that later they met for a coffee and one of them said that he liked the blue and white color of the house, but didn't like the fact that there were two windows and no door. The second person said that he also liked the blue and white colors of that house, but pointed out that his friend was wrong and there was a door between the two windows. The third person looked confused and insisted that there was only one big window and no door. The fourth person explained that it was not a big window, but a big balcony.

They argued this way for some time, all perfectly sure about their side of the story (their side of the house), feeling righteous and disappointed that others did not agree with them or did not SEE their point of view.

The truth is, we ALL filter out reality through our perceptions and beliefs, which often do not match the perceptions and beliefs of another person, and when that happens disappointment and arguments set in. Most of the time, there are no right or wrong sides. Just like in the example above, all four friends defended what they saw and understood. The problem is, none of them could see the full picture.

When we do our best to see other points of view, many arguments can be avoided. Even if from our perspective, based on where we are in our lives at the moment, we still do not 'see' someone's point of view, we can just give it the benefit of the doubt, and instead of working hard to prove that we are right and they are wrong, let it go.

Action Steps

- If someone is important to you and it is important for you that he or she understands how you feel and what you believe about a particular issue, explain it calmly without blaming, belittling, aggression, or self-pity.
- If the other person is attacking you in order to feed on your reaction, neutralize the situation by ignoring their rudeness or their attack. What they do and how they behave is their problem. When a dog barks, you don't bark back. If you react, you join them in the ego game where everyone loses.
- Remind yourself of the house example above and give the other person benefit of the doubt.
- Sometimes it is better to agree to disagree and amiably remain with individual points of view. Who said that people have to agree on everything? Life would be very boring if they did.

PART 3

UNDERSTAND AND BOOST YOUR FEEL-GOOD EMOTIONS

CHAPTER 34

CHOOSING TO FEEL GOOD ON A REGULAR BASIS

What do you usually wish for someone on their birthday? What wishes do you usually have for your own birthday?

Most people's wishes for each other are standard – health, happiness, love, abundance, and success.

To the above, many also add for themselves the wish to have freedom, peace of mind, and a sense of achievement. They want to feel passionate and motivated doing what they love to do; and they want to feel contentment, joy, and gratitude.

We crave intimacy, connection, adventure, expression of our creativity, and our abilities. We also want to feel understood, valued, respected, and needed.

We seek mostly the expressions of the above through others and often we succeed. But, the success in this case is always temporary and elusive and when we do finally get what we want, we live in the fear of losing it.

This section is dedicated to the feel-good emotions. In the ideal world, we might want to experience them one hundred percent of the time and when people reach a state of enlightenment – when they are able to silence the ego and the mind, they are able to silence their craving for all of the emotions except love and peace of mind, which are then not really emotions but the states of their Being.

However, for now, when ego is still playing a big part in our lives, it is best not to fight it but to work with it. If you could shift the ratio of feel-good emotions to feel-bad emotions to 80/20 (instead of the other way around as most people live right now), how would the experience of your life be different?

Choosing to Feel Good on a Regular Basis | 75

> ### Action Steps
>
> - As you read through this section of feel-good emotions, remind yourself that when it comes to manifesting them in your life, don't wait for something outside of you to happen so that one day, when it does, you can experience them.
> - First, be clear what each emotion means to you and how you would personally like to feel it and experience it.
> - Second, feel that emotion on a regular basis and THEN you will manifest circumstances, people, and experiences where those emotions will dominate.

CHAPTER 35

THE PLEASURE OF FEELING HEALTHY

I assume that everyone, at least everyone reading this book, understands the importance of good health and that without it, nothing else matters. This is the reason why we always wish it to each other regardless of the race, cultural or religious upbringing, or social status. When I ask people their highest values, health is usually up there.

But here is an interesting observation… Though most people believe they value health more than other things, their actions, more often than not, prove differently.

We know the basic rules of good health, vitality, high energy and longevity – eat right, exercise regularly, think positively, get enough rest and reduce the level of stress. And yet, most people do not get enough sleep, often eat food or combine different foods in a way that is upsetting to their bodies and their energy levels, even when they have the information about it. Most people do not exercise enough and do not take the actions that they know would reduce their levels of stress and anxiety.

It is human nature to choose the way of least resistance and effort. If nothing is really bothering us at the moment, or not bothering us badly enough, we choose the easy way. As soon as something serious happens, when we feel that our life or something else that is very important to us is on the line, we suddenly get motivated to take action. *Reacting rather than preventing.*

The Pleasure of Feeling Healthy | 77

> **Action Steps**
>
> - If you are one of the people who reacts rather than prevents, it is time to reevaluate what is, basically, a habit.
> - If it has been a while since you had a medical check-up, make an appointment today and don't wait until life forces you to do that. Regular physical check-ups as well regular visits to a dentist, can save you a lot of money and a lot of pain in the future. But you already know that. I am just here to give you a gentle reminder.
> - Write down 21 action steps you can take to improve your health physically, mentally, and emotionally. Choose from that list five new steps you can implement each month to create new empowering habits.

CHAPTER 36

THE PLEASURE OF FEELING CONFIDENT

Who do you think about when you think of a confident person? What makes that person confident, in your opinion?

To me, people who are confident tend to be more inspiring, optimistic, self-assured, charismatic, captivating, enthusiastic, passionate, and authentic than those who are less confident. They believe they will win when playing, take more risks, think more abstractly, and have a certain presence about themselves that attracts others.

I haven't met a person yet who told me, "Well, I'd rather not be confident." Confidence is a desired characteristic to have and for a good reason – our level of confidence in any particular area of our life is directly related to the level of success we can achieve in that area.

Confidence is our ability to deal with whatever life brings our way. It is our belief that we can overcome obstacles in an effective resourceful way, no matter what they are.

A confident person is also someone who likes himself or herself and knows that no matter what happens, they have inner resources to overcome it.

Confidence increases with experience and repetition. The more we do something, the better we become at it, and the more confident we feel.

Another relatively easy way to increase confidence is by changing your physiology. By physiology I mean your posture, how you walk, and the way you use your body in general. Think for a moment about the physiology of a confident person. Now imagine someone who shows a lack of confidence just by how they stand, sit, walk, and talk. What is the difference?

By keeping your spine straight, shoulders back, and holding your head high – by adopting the physiology of confidence, you start feeling more confident and eventually program yourself to BE more confident on a regular basis.

Action Steps

- Spend the next day paying attention to how you walk – walk with a straight spine, head held high, and in a slower, more conscious tempo. Speak slower and deeper. Listen more than you speak. Notice how it makes you feel, if other people react differently to you, and if you achieve different results.
- If you like what you experience, practice the physiology of confidence at all times.
- To fully accept and like yourself, stop comparing, judging, belittling yourself, practicing self-abuse, and giving into fear.
- Finally, do the things you fear. The more fears and obstacles you overcome, the more confident you will become.

CHAPTER 37

THE PLEASURE OF FEELING VALUED

Rabbi Simon Jacobson in his book, *Towards a Meaningful Life* asks this question, *"Do you know what children need more than anything else?"* He answers this question by saying that, *"It's not gifts or places to travel to. It's not even time. It's validation. The acknowledgement that when they see the look in the eyes of a parent, they get the message that they're important. That they are valuable."*

The need to feel valuable does not disappear when we grow up. It is a human core need and you have the ability and the power to give a gift of validation to yourself and to those around you.

"Our core emotional need is to feel valued. Without a stable sense of value, we don't know who we are and we don't feel safe in the world." Tony Schwartz, president and CEO of The Energy Project

When someone doesn't return your phone call or ignores your message; when you feel that someone is taking advantage of you or using you; when your hard work and efforts are not being acknowledged, it triggers a sense of threat and danger.

Unfortunately, many people strive to achieve a sense of value by putting other people down so that they would feel superior. To them, the achievements of others equals their failure. This ego-driven behavior only makes people feel more insecure but in their unconscious attempt to survive, they proceed to do it again and again.

When we move away from the demands and hungers of the ego, we are able to fulfill our need to be valued in a way that doesn't create comparisons and judgements.

Action Steps

- Nobody can make you feel anything without your consent. If someone's words or behavior upsets you or triggers a reaction, examine your own beliefs of yourself in that area.
- If you are secure about your worthiness and value in this world, nobody can make you feel otherwise; therefore, when a person comes into your life and triggers those emotions, be grateful to him or her because they are here to point out to you where the work needs to be done.

CHAPTER 38

THE PLEASURE OF BEING IN A LOVING RELATIONSHIP

One of the main goals of being in a loving relationship is to experience connection, happiness, and a sense of fulfilment and completeness. However, when this doesn't happen, especially if it doesn't happen more than once, we get disappointed and disillusioned.

But, what if we changed our expectations of the purpose of being in a relationship?

What if we saw each relationship as an opportunity to make you more conscious? An opportunity to bring to the surface emotions, which are simply reflected in our partner – emotions that can, at each moment, come to the light and be released or transformed, changing your pattern of behavior, your future experiences in life, and your destiny.

We have been conditioned to fit into a story which someone else has created for us, of how a relationship should be. We are conditioned to believe that all relationships are meant to exist and to function "till death do them part," and if it doesn't happen, if we do not fit into this paradigm, or any other for that matter, we suffer…thinking that we have failed.

Why not then, write your own script of what a loving relationship is?

Imagine that you wake up and next to you is your ideal partner. What qualities would that partner have? Imagine in detail as your day progresses. What do you do? How do you feel? In what way does your relationship enriches the experience of your life?

Action Steps

- Write down a vision as described above in the present tense as if it is happening right now.
- Examine the qualities you have described for your partner. Do you possess those qualities yourself? *We usually attract people who reflect back to us who we are, and who vibrate at the same frequency we do.*
- Even if you are already in a relationship, write that vision with your partner in mind. Our expectations create our reality.
- Always begin with your own growth and improvement and do not try to change the other person. Everything around you changes to match your new vibration, including the behavior of the people around you.

CHAPTER 39

THE PLEASURE OF FEELING CONNECTED

Some connections are based on lack and neediness and, when those connections are made, they reinforce these distractive emotions. The loss of those connections cause us suffering as we feel the void and rush to fill it.

However, true connections are made when we open our hearts to the experience and feel fully present. These connections can last a moment or some can last years but each carries a gift of expansion and new beginnings and when they are gone, there is no pain, only gratitude. In fact, I believe that one of the main purposes of a human experience is the ability to fearlessly make and to keep these connections.

Unfortunately, the majority of people put up blocks and protections, afraid to let anyone close to their hearts in fear of becoming vulnerable to rejection and loss. As all fears, this is an insecurity-based reaction and keeps us living in duality and delusion.

The more we block ourselves from true connections, intimacy, and love, the more we crave them. The masks we put on and the pretend games we play with ourselves as a defense mechanism might feel true for a while, but eventually our soul's desire and need to connect either leads us to open our hearts and let our true nature blossom, dissolving fear and defenses, or it reinforces Ego's defenses which then lead to building stronger walls, leaving us in greater misery and fear.

Action Steps

- Start by establishing a true connection with your own self. This is done by listening to what your body and your emotions are telling you.
- Find a way to connect to nature on a regular basis. Spend time in nature, notice the perfection and the beauty of it. Feel One with it.
- When you feel strong and connected within, making heart-felt connections with other people becomes easy and fearless. The fear of rejection vanishes as you understand your true value and realize that no one can reject or possess you.

CHAPTER 40

THE PLEASURE OF FEELING FREE

One of the top values for most people is freedom. If this is one of your values, have you ever stopped and thought what it means to you? *What does it really mean to be free?*

Of course, it means different things to different people and it is important for you to define it for yourself in order to create it.

For me, freedom means to be myself at all times. To achieve this kind of freedom, one must be clear about their values and boundaries and not worry about living up to other people's expectations and opinions.

Freedom to me also means to be free of negative beliefs, habits, and thoughts. Just imagine for one moment what life would feel like if you are able to transform beliefs, habits, thoughts, and emotions that are holding you back? How free would you feel?

Now imagine feeling free to do what you want, when you want, and in the style you choose. How would that feel? What needs to happen for you to achieve this kind of freedom?

How free would you feel if you let go of your goals and desires?

How free would you feel if you let go of control and allowed life to happen, trusting the Universe and yourself in your ability to do exactly what needs to be done as it comes without planning, controlling, and stressing over every detail?

Action Steps

- Think about the above probing questions regarding freedom. Which resonate with you most?
- Define freedom for yourself. Make it achievable within and not through the outside sources.
- Everything starts within and everything is in your control when you are willing to *take full responsibility for where you are in your journey of life and your ability to take it where you want to go.*

CHAPTER 41

THE PLEASURE OF FEELING PROSPEROUS AND ABUNDANT

Feelings of prosperity and abundance are often not equal to the amount of money someone has or earns. There are many wealthy people, by most standards, who feel scarcity and lack on a regular basis. They live in fear of losing. On the other side, of course, there are many people, whom many would consider very poor, who feel prosperous and abundant.

But philosophy aside, if one of your goals is to become more prosperous than you are right now and to live in abundance, then the first thing to realize is that we do not so much create abundance as tune into it.

Tuning into abundance means energetically vibrating at the same frequency as abundance is. How do we do that?

First, by observing that working hard does not always guarantee prosperity. How many hardworking people do you know who are still struggling? It is also not about the level of education. And nether it is about gender, upbringing, age, or intelligence.

It is however, about your mindset and in this case, your prosperity mindset – your attitudes, beliefs, thoughts, and feelings about money and prosperity in general.

If wealth and prosperity are your goals, observe people whom you consider prosperous and wealthy. Read their biographies, listen to their interviews, talk to them if possible, ask if they can be your mentor, and basically do all you can to understand *their* mindset on this topic.

In fact, immerse yourself in this topic as much as possible and at the same time have fun with it and do not block the flow with worry and doubt by putting too much importance.

Finally, love yourself enough to know that you deserve to have abundance in your life. Abundance is your birthright. Feel comfortable with it within and only then you can experience it in your life.

Action Steps

- Notice how abundant and wealthy you are already.
- Abundance does not manifest itself just financially – we can feel abundant and prosperous when we observe the magnificence of nature, the happiness of those we love, the health we might be lucky enough to have, and the miracles that happen in our lives on a regular basis, if we take the time to stop and notice them.
- Tune into abundance by feeling abundant.
- It goes without saying that you don't just sit there dreaming about being wealthy. Take action that is presented to you by the Universe and when hard work is required, invest your energy and effort into it.
- Have fun as you bring value to others and see how your value and your abundance grow with it.

CHAPTER 42

THE PLEASURE OF FEELING BEAUTIFUL

Imagine someone saying to you from the heart, *"You are so beautiful!"* or *"You have such beautiful eyes,"* or *"You have a beautiful smile."* Imagine looking in the mirror and thinking to yourself, *"Wow, you* are *beautiful!"*

Do you ever catch yourself saying that to your own reflection? Do you consider yourself beautiful? Do you hear people telling you often how beautiful you are as they look at you with admiration?

If not, would you want to?

I am a firm believer that beauty comes from within. *It is in our energy*, in the way our eyes sparkle, in the way we enjoy and appreciate life.

Most of all, it is in the way we appreciate our own beauty and the beauty around us – the beauty of the people we come in contact with, the beauty of nature, of art, of music, and, of course, the beauty of our own thoughts.

When we notice all that is beautiful and we absorb that energy, that energy in return transforms us, making us look younger, more beautiful and very attractive to others, regardless of our physical features, our age, or our socio-economic status.

When we feel beautiful, it doesn't mean that we are narcissistic or self-absorbed. It means that we appreciate who we are and accept ourselves just as we are, finding beauty in all imperfections that make us unique.

Action Steps

- If you want to feel beautiful, don't wait for someone to compliment you. As with everything else, feel beautiful first and then everyone around you will see that beauty and react to it.
- *Notice* the beauty around you – see it in the flowers, in the trees, in the animals, in the architecture, art, music, and dance.
- Beauty is all around us if we pay attention to it. And when we give something our focused attention, we absorb the essence of it and it becomes part of who we are.

CHAPTER 43

THE PLEASURE OF FEELING HAPPY

If you take any one of your goals and keep asking yourself why you want to achieve it, you will eventually get to the same answer as most people do – "Because I want to be happy!"

We strive for happiness and yet happiness is an elusive state of being that is inconsistent and difficult to hold on to, especially when our means of getting into that state depend on the sources outside of ourselves – things, other people, opportunities, places to live or to visit, etc.

When we search for happiness outside of ourselves, it never lasts. In fact, *searching* for happiness in itself means that you do not accept the current situation and that you do not feel happy at the moment.

When you search for something or strive for something, you remain in that vibration – the vibration of: "One day I will get there and will be happy." When we focus on something that we want in the future, it will always remain in the future, as demonstrated so well in the example below.

There is a sign in one of the Irish pubs that says, *"Free Beer Tomorrow!"* Do you think anyone is ever able to collect that free beer? The answer is obviously "No" because tomorrow never comes. You can only change your reality by doing something different in the moment.

Therefore, as Leo Tolstoy observed, *"If you want to be happy, BE."*

There is no other way to lasting true happiness. *It is a choice.* And it is a choice you can make right now and every moment after that.

Action Steps

- Think back to the moments in your life, in the last few weeks, that made you feel very happy. Write them down.
- Next time when you are feeling not as happy, read them and remember what it felt like. The more you shift your focus to being and to feeling happy, the more you attract situations that manifest that emotion.
- You are 'allowed' not to feel happy at times. We are not robots and forcing happiness never works. Just allow the unwanted feeling to pass without dwelling in it and your natural state of happiness and wellbeing will return.

CHAPTER 44

THE PLEASURE OF FEELING PEACE OF MIND

What does it feel like to have a peace of mind?

Actually, peace of mind, just as love, is not really an emotion triggered by some good thoughts. *Peace of mind is the absence of thoughts.*

As Peter McWilliams wisely observed, *"If you want peace, stop fighting. If you want peace of mind, stop fighting with your thoughts."*

When we remain 'unconscious' and allow thoughts to take over, our emotions become uncontrollable and peace of mind becomes an abstract ideal and an unachievable dream.

The constant chatter in our heads at times feels like an untamed beast, taking over our ability to sleep well, to make clear decisions, and to appreciate each and every moment as we live it.

People who are able to stop fighting their thoughts, judging them, giving energy and importance to them, associate with them…people who are able to separate themselves from who they are and what they are feeling and thinking, are the people who are able to find peace of mind.

"Ego says, 'Once everything falls into place, I'll feel peace'. Spirit says, 'Find your peace, and then everything will fall into place'." Marianne Williamson

Action Steps

- Do not take ownership of the thoughts that are passing by. Remember, there is you and there are thoughts. You can choose to dwell in them or you can choose to let them float past.
- Use the thoughts but do not become possessed by them.
- It is a misconception that best ideas or solutions come because we think a lot about them. They come when we are able to stop the thinking noise in our heads and listen to the inner voice of intuition and higher consciousness.
- Therefore, you are not wasting your time when you are not thinking, as many learned to believe; you are actually allowing yourself to tap into the higher consciousness of most creative solutions and ideas.
- Let go of wanting to control the process, just allow it to happen and witness how much easier and faster everything begins to fall into place.

CHAPTER 45

THE PLEASURE OF FEELING GRATITUDE

I would like to finish this section with a chapter on gratitude because in my opinion it is an emotion that makes everything we want possible; it is an emotion with which everything ends and everything starts.

Think about what made you feel grateful in the last few days? What are you feeling grateful for right now?

Usually people feel grateful when something they really wanted has come to fruition or when they were able to avoid an unwanted outcome. People feel grateful when they realize that they have been blessed with what they have or some people who are there for them in their lives. They also feel grateful for the beauty that surrounds them and many other things that they happen to have or experience in their lives right now.

But what if you were to feel grateful for what you desire but don't have yet?

If you want more money and abundance, feel grateful for all that you already have and are able to buy. If you want to be in better shape, feel grateful for the fact that you love yourself enough to want to change that and that you are taking action in that direction, appreciating your body and your health in the process. If you want to be loved, be grateful for all the people who already love you and for your ability to give love and to receive love.

Because the more we feel grateful, the more we attract into our lives things and situations that reinforce that emotion; and the more we tell ourselves that there isn't much in our lives to be grateful for on a regular basis, the more we remain stuck in that place.

Action Steps

- Start a Gratitude Journal, if you haven't already, and write down ten things you are grateful for every single day.
- At the end of each year, write down at least 21 best memories of that year.
- Think of at least one person in your life right now that matters a lot to you and write 21 reasons why you feel grateful for having that person in your life. Share the list with that person and his or her life will transform as well.

PART 4

MASTERING YOUR EMOTIONS- MASTERING YOUR LIFE

Emotional Growth

Anger

Jealousy

Bitterness

Disappointment

CHAPTER 46

WHAT DOES IT MEAN TO MASTER YOUR EMOTIONS?

Awareness and understanding of the nature of emotions, as well as knowledge and skill of releasing them, or simply not attaching yourself to them, is what makes you the master, rather than a slave, to your emotions.

By nature of emotions I mean that it is important to always remember that you and the emotions you experience are different entities and should not be personalized. This understanding is required in order to be able to release unwanted emotions or simply to not attach yourself to them in the first place.

It is also important to understand that emotions are often triggered by learned behaviors from past experiences. They are also triggered by the life stories we create for ourselves. When our experiences do not match our stories, negative emotions are triggered.

Some emotions are just floating by and do not need our focus or our attention. Some emotions come to make us aware of a pattern that doesn't serve us anymore or a life story that has expired.

In this section of the book, you will find the information on how to work with your emotions – how to make them your best friends, rather than your enemies and something to hide from or to push away. You will gain an understanding of how to stop being scared of strong emotions and learn to either express them when necessary or release them when you are ready through different techniques that work best for you.

Action Steps

- Next time an emotion arises in you, just observe it. Do not attach yourself to it right away.
- Ask yourself, "Is this emotion triggered by a past experience and an old pattern? What purpose does it serve? Do I want to explore it deeper or should I just ignore it?"
- When you just ignore a passing emotion, it cannot survive and just dissipates. Realize though, that ignoring an emotion – not giving it your focus, is not the same as pushing away an emotion to which you are already attached.
- If the same emotion keeps coming, it means you have attached yourself to it and need to release it. You will learn how to release emotions in this section.

CHAPTER 47

YOU ARE NOT YOUR STORY

Well, you actually are, or at least your experience of yourself and what happens to you is consistent with the story you have subconsciously created for yourself.

At some point in your life you have concluded whether you are good looking or not; charismatic or not; capable or not; a good dancer or someone with two left feet; too fat, too skinny, or just right; shy or outgoing; sporty or lazy; romantic or not really; lucky or someone who attracts trouble.

We create a story with each new romantic encounter too, and then get disappointed with something or someone who doesn't live up to it. We try to change ourselves or the other person, even our children to match the stories that we create.

And then, if or when things don't work out, we grieve not just losing someone, but also the end of the story that didn't have its happy ending and didn't go according to the script.

All this happens on a deeply subconscious level unless we "wake up" and become an observer of our self-created scripts rather than get sucked into them, mistaking them for the reality.

Action Steps

- Remember that you are always in control and that you are not just the main character that you get to play but you are also the writer, the director and the producer of all your life stories.
- If one of the stories you have created for yourself has taken a life of its own and took a wrong turn making you unhappy in the process, all you need to do is rewrite it. You can fire some supporting actors and hire new ones, you can change how the main character, which of course is you, reacts to what is happening... You can do anything your heart desires except keeping yourself stuck in a movie that doesn't work for you anymore.
- Take a few minutes to rewrite one of your outdated old stories or just throw that one away and write down a whole new one. Refer to the example in the next chapter.

CHAPTER 48

HOW TO FREE YOURSELF FROM THE STORIES WHICH DON'T SERVE YOU ANYMORE

We cannot create change by fighting the existing reality. To experience something different, we need to design a new reality that makes the one we don't want to experience anymore obsolete.

When we don't like what we see, it is entirely up to us to change it. When our story and the role we play in it changes, so does our experience of a perceived reality.

One practical and easily-implementable way to free yourself from old and expired stories is to basically rewrite them.

First, you need to write down your story regarding a particular situation – describe your reality as it is and how you feel at the moment. Second, you need to write a new story on what is happening, but as you would want it to be.

For example, Eric's current situation, his current experience in life, or his current story, is that his partner just doesn't get him – she is incapable of understanding why he feels the way he feels. Eric gets frustrated with his partner for not understanding him and he gets frustrated with himself for feeling incapable of explaining.

It bothers him deeply that they argue constantly and these arguments make him feel like a failure, forcing him to consider separation, even though they still love each other and he doesn't want to complicate his life by starting it all over again and jeopardizing the lives of other people who are involved. He feels stuck, stressed, and unhappy.

Even though the above example might seem to Eric as very real, it is important to always be reminded that it is just an illusion – a creation, an energetic manifestation of the past thoughts, intentions and actions. Therefore, the best way to change it, is by stepping outside and rewriting the script, creating a different illusion based on new thoughts, expectations, and actions. So with that in mind, Eric might want to rewrite his story as follows:

"I finally found a way to communicate my needs to my partner. I did it by putting my needs aside for a while and reaching out to her. When I understood what was really bothering her, I realized that we were basically reflecting each other's pain and frustration and by giving to her what she needed, I started to feel a lot more fulfilled in a relationship myself. Almost like magic, arguments dissipated and we are now eager to please each other and to bring happiness to each other every single day. We speak only with respect to each other and take time to talk and to understand each other's needs. I can't remember the last time I felt so loved and so connected. I go to sleep with a sense of peace and contentment and I wake up with a smile on my face feeling proud of myself for finding a way to make this work and bringing back stability and happiness to our household."

Action Steps

- The new story created by Eric might be far from the experience of his current reality at this moment, but by writing it down, clarifying exactly what he wants to experience, he has now created this possible outcome of the situation and rather than just reacting, he can now keep this vision in mind, knowing that it is possible, and eventually manifesting it into his new reality.
- Now it is your turn to rewrite one of your stories.

CHAPTER 49

HOW AND WHY WE FILTER OUR REALITY

We will always experience a reality of which we feel worthy and which we are ready to experience based on where we feel we fit in this world.

The stories we create for ourselves do not just influence our present and our future, they also distort what has happened to us in the past, often taking us far from the truth of reality, in the subconscious attempt of self-preservation.

Our minds are so powerful that if what happened to us in the past did not support our current story, we would subconsciously alter the events of what has already happened to the point that we would believe it actually happened that way.

People who give themselves a role of a victim in their stories, would alter their past and influence their present and their future to support this role and to prove to themselves and to others that they are and have been the victims. People who give themselves a role of a hero, would do the same and so on.

We so desperately want to hold on to our stories of ourselves that anyone trying to point out anything different, even when it's the truth, is met with strong resistance, which usually leads to arguments, disagreements, and at times irreversible break-ups in relationships.

When you react to criticism or feel that you constantly need to defend yourself, your point of view, or your behavior, it means that you do not accept yourself for who you are. Trying to prove something to another is basically trying to prove it to yourself.

Ability to take criticism lightly and constructively indicates a level of confidence and security in yourself in the area being criticized. If you catch yourself reacting, take it as a message to look within and heal that part of your life instead of getting hurt or upset with the one who criticizes. People usually criticize due to their own low level of self-esteem and as soon as you stop reacting and feeding their ego, they will see no reason to keep on.

How and Why We Filter Our Reality | **107**

Action Steps

- What in your current reality makes you happy?
- What in your current reality would you like to be different?
- What do you feel is stopping you from manifesting those changes?
- Your reality will change only when you are ready to change on every level – when the old unwanted reality becomes painful enough to give you the courage to make the necessary changes.

CHAPTER 50

HOW TO CONSCIOUSLY PROGRAM YOURSELF

"*Until you make the unconscious conscious, it will direct your life and you will call it fate.*" C.G. Jung

One way to consciously program yourself and to guide your thoughts, which in turn create your emotions, is by using affirmations – statements that help you program or reprogram your subconscious to help you achieve what you desire. Examples of affirmations would include:

- My life is a masterpiece and I am the artist.
- I am complete.
- I feel safe, supported, and cherished.
- I have enough; I am enough; I do enough.

You also consciously program yourself to have the kind of future that you want to have by writing down the vision of your future. Writing down your long-term vision is one of the most exciting and rewarding past-times – it is a time when you become a Creator, your own God or Goddess and you create your life exactly as YOU want it to be.

I recommend writing a long-term vision of your life describing a moment in it three or five years from now. It is believed that we tend to overestimate what we can achieve in one year and underestimate what we can achieve in five.

Action Steps

- Find, or better create, some free uninterrupted time for yourself, let your imagination go and write down your perfect life.
- It is important to know that just as any computer programming, when programming yourself, whether through affirmations, creative visualizations, or vision boards, it is necessary to follow certain rules. So please review the rules of writing a vision as well as writing your affirmations and your goals as described in the next chapter.

CHAPTER 51

FIVE RULES OF MIND PROGRAMING FOR AFFIRMATIONS, GOALS AND VISION WRITING

PRESENT TENSE

It is important to write your vision, goals, and your affirmations in the present tense – as if it is happening right now or has already happened. Remember the sign in the Irish pub *"Free Beer Tomorrow?"*

When we make our goals in the future (i.e. I will be happy), it always stays in the future. Instead, say, "I am happy."

PERSONAL

Both vision and affirmations need to be written from the point of view of the person who is writing it. Affirmations therefore, will start with an 'I'. In the vision, everything is also revolving around the person who is writing it and how everything and everyone in it makes the writer feel.

The reason why you want to write your vision in such a way, is because you can only change yourself and your reaction to things. When you change, everything and everyone around you changes, or, moves out of your life to be replaced by someone or something that fits the new vibration of your new life.

POSITIVE

When writing your vision and affirmations, use only positive statements. Rather than saying "I am not fat," you want to say, "I am slim" or "I am fit" or "I am healthy." This is because the brain doesn't register a negative command. If I ask you, "Don't think of red shoes on the cow," what will you immediately think about?

PRECISE AND REPEATED REGULARLY

For the affirmations to work, make them precise and repeat them regularly. I recommend choosing three affirmations for 10 days. For the duration of those 10 days, repeat each affirmation 10 times just before you go to sleep and

10 time when you wake up. Then choose new affirmations or leave the ones you feel you need to give more focus to.

Vision doesn't need to be repeated constantly. Vision is more of a destination that you create and let go of control in terms of how it will happen. Affirmations on the other hand will help you become the kind of person that will attract your perfect vision.

USE EMOTION

If you repeat your affirmations one hundred times like a parrot without any emotions, they would not work.

As you repeat your affirmations, visualize what it would be like, really feel it! Feel what it is like to really love yourself as you say "I love myself", feel what it is like to have enough and to be enough, if that is what you are affirming. Put emotion into it and when you can, say it out loud.

When writing a vision, always include emotions. How would you feel when you have that perfect house or a car? How would you feel when you are free to do what you want and when you want? What would it feel like to be accepted just as you are and to be loved unconditionally?

We cannot create that which we cannot conceptualize and imagine what it would be like. So take the time to feel and express your emotions because *it is emotions that program us.*

CHAPTER 52

I LIKE MYSELF

One of the most important affirmations for anyone to use on a regular basis is

- *I like myself!*

This is because our level of success in anything that we choose to do is directly related to our level of self-esteem in that area.

You can try hundreds of diets but if deep inside you don't like yourself, you will keep putting the weight back on. If you don't feel you deserve to be loved, you would find yourself heartbroken over and over again and if you don't value yourself or don't respect yourself, you would get disrespect from others and would feel that you are underpaid and undervalued at work and at home.

When I started working with this affirmation, I was surprised how uncomfortable I felt saying it. I didn't feel there was congruency and deep belief and it surprised me at the time as I had to face a painful truth – I didn't really like myself.

After a while, and certainly now, saying "I like myself," feels the same as saying "it is sunny outside," when it is sunny outside. I don't feel like I am pretending, I know deep down that I do like myself and the repetition of this affirmation has helped me believe and act consistently with this new reality.

Action Steps

- As with all affirmations, repeat "I like myself," ten times as you wake up and ten times just before you fall asleep. Really feel it as you are saying it. Do it for ten consecutive days.
- Repeat this affirmation regularly as you look at yourself in the mirror.

CHAPTER 53

I AM ONE

Another very important affirmation is
* *I am One*

Repeating this affirmation has a transformational and transcending effect. I like to say it when I start feeling stressed or disconnected.

For example, repeating this affirmation has helped me move through traffic faster, manifest successful outcomes of meetings, and put things in perspective when a particular situation would start dragging me down.

Feeling ONE with yourself, with the people around you and your immediate environment, as well as with the whole universe, has a very grounding and calming effect, too.

Let me share with you one of my favorite meditations. I love it because it is very short (it only takes three breaths) and because it is one of the most effective I've ever used.

Sit with your back straight and your legs and arms uncrossed. Close your eyes, take a deep breath and as you breathe out, mentally say "three" and relax all the muscles on your body from head to toes…

Take another deep breath and this time mentally say "two" and release all thoughts, worries, concerns… just let it go for now…

Now take your third deep breath and say "one", as you say it feel one with yourself, the people in your immediate environment, the room you are in, and the universe.

Open your eyes and feel how much calmer and more peaceful you are.

Action Steps

- When you see a beautiful tender flower, say "I am One."
- When you see a powerful and magnificent mountain, say "I am One."
- When you see an abundant and tranquil ocean, say "I am One."
- Think of the qualities you would like to have when you are in nature and repeat this affirmation. It will help you create those qualities within you and will help you stay connected, centered, and tranquil.

CHAPTER 54

THE DANGEROUS HABIT OF THINKING

"*Not to be able to stop thinking is a dreadful affliction, but we don't realize this because almost everybody is suffering from it, so it is considered normal.*" Eckhart Tolle

Did you know that most of us are thinking over 60,000 thoughts per day? And most of these 60,000 thoughts are the same as the thoughts we were thinking the day before, and the day before that?

Those 60,000 thoughts that we are thinking are responsible for triggering your emotions, which then create your experience and determine the quality of your life, essentially creating your destiny.

If you are not able to disconnect your mind and silence your thoughts for more than a few seconds, you are a slave to your mind and it controls you rather than you being in control of it.

Let me ask you, what do you fear might happen if you stop thinking?

Do you feel you might lose your identity, your sense of self? Will not be able to function adequately in this world? Or that life will lose its meaning?

Constant thinking is just a habit, an addiction without which we feel we cannot survive. Fortunately, like any other habits, it is possible to transform or to change it when we let go of the fear of doing so.

"*There is nothing either good or bad, but thinking makes it so.*" Shakespeare

Action Steps

As discussed in the chapter above, we rarely find creative solutions to our problems by thinking; we find them by silencing our mind.

- The first step, is to be open-minded enough to agree or at least to test the above statement.
- Second, start disconnecting your mind from the relentless flow of thoughts little by little. For example, when you are in the shower, give your full focus to the water and how it feels running down your body. Connect with the water and disconnect from the thoughts. Then, when you can disconnect even for five minutes, add to it while doing other tasks.
- The best way to disconnect from the flow of thoughts is by giving your full focus to what is happening at this moment – your breathing, the way you walk, the trees and flowers around you, the clouds in the sky, etc.

CHAPTER 55

MEDITATION MADE EASY

Most people have heard enough about the importance and the benefits of meditation; unfortunately, the majority of people in the Western part of the world seem to have difficulties with understanding what meditation is, how to do it, and when to find the time for it.

As I have mentioned earlier, I used to be what is known as a type A personality, always on the go, doing many things at once, planning, thinking, creating, and having no clue what it means to just sit in one place and at the same time not do anything and especially not think about anything.

So I am one of those people who can confidently tell you – if I can do it, so can you. If I could make meditation my daily practice, so can you. In fact, I can't imagine my life flowing as it flows now and my much calmer and much more confident way of being without my meditation practices.

By practicing meditation, you get access to the answers of your questions much more effectively than if you try to analyze or think them through. You also have the power to eliminate obstacles that are now preventing you from living your life masterpiece.

Through meditation you work seamlessly as ONE with your higher self and with the Universe and, when this happens, there is no stopping you!

For example, if one of your goals is to have peace of mind, as it is for most people I've spoken to, meditation can help you achieve that. As Les Brown, motivational speaker and radio and TV host, has observed,

"With peace of mind you can create wealth, but wealth cannot buy peace of mind. You have to create that from within."

And so is everything else is created from within before it can be manifested and experienced in your reality.

Action Steps

- If you want to start practicing meditation right away but not sure what to do or whom to ask for help, I recommend guided meditations that can be found easily on YouTube. There are specific guided meditations on specific issue, such as meditations for people who can't stop thinking, or for people who can't fall asleep; meditations for anxiety, for positive energy, for overcoming fear, for detachment and so on.
- Find the ones that work for you. You don't need to sit in a special pose to begin with, you can lay down comfortably and fall asleep if you want. What is important is that you start disconnecting from the mental noise of the daily problem-solving and learn to just be.
- With time, as you make meditation your habit, you can learn how to sit in a position where your spine is completely straight and the energy flows easily from the top of your head to the base of your spine, and you can learn to switch off all your thoughts and go within easily and quickly.

CHAPTER 56

A WORD ON HYPNOSIS

I am a certified clinical hypnotherapist and can say with confidence that hypnosis is a wonderful tool to access subconscious mind and address all kinds of issues, such as weight loss, smoking secession, pain relief, accessing forgotten memory, releasing unwanted emotions, as well as understanding and healing emotional or physical traumas in a relaxed and painless way.

Being in a state of hypnosis is not much different to being in a state of deep relaxation. It is a meditative state where our awareness of our physical environment is diminished and our awareness of our inner state is heightened. It is through carefully chosen suggestions in this heightened state of awareness that therapy takes place.

Most myths associated with hypnotherapy are false. Myths such as not being able to wake up, losing control and doing or saying something we don't really want, or not being able to be hypnotized because of the highly active brain.

Briefly, everyone can be hypnotized because all hypnosis is self-hypnosis; however, if someone really doesn't want to be hypnotized, they won't be. Another important fact, is that in a state of hypnosis we will never do or say anything against our will because of our heightened awareness of all that is going on while we are in that state. Finally, it is impossible not to wake up from hypnosis. Even though people think they fall asleep in the middle of the session, they don't – hypnosis is a state where a person is neither wide-awake nor asleep, but somewhere in between.

This is a powerful state that allows deep relaxation, accelerated learning opportunity, accessing forgotten memory, and mind training. It is a state through which we all move in and out at least one hundred times a day when we attend to activities that do not require thinking, such as brushing teeth, driving, walking in nature, painting, etc.

"The human mind is a channel through which things-to-be are coming into the realm of things-that-are." Henry Ford

Action Steps

If you choose to do a hypnotherapy session because there is a particular emotion that is really stuck or you feel that accessing your subconscious can be helpful to resolve an issue that doesn't want to go away, this is what you can expect:

- During the hypnotherapy session the therapist will talk to you in depth to understand the nature of your issue and the final outcome you would like to achieve.
- The next step would be to help you relax completely. Through positive suggestions, based on what was discussed previously, the therapist will then guide you to access your subconscious to either get the information that you need or to use positive suggestions to help you get a different perspective on a particular issue.
- After the session is concluded, the client usually feels refreshed and armed with new understanding and new tools to resolve what needs to be resolved.

CHAPTER 57

STOP THE DRAMA

"*Most people are in love with their particular life drama. Their story is their identity.*" Eckhart Tolle

We create drama in our lives because it brings meaning. It gives us a sense of purpose. It makes us feel alive because of all the emotions we get bombarded with.

Is it wrong to attract drama? No. Nothing is really wrong or right and who is to judge anyway? Drama is most people's comfort zone and there is an element of satisfaction that people experience when they are in it or when they get to resolve it.

However, a time will come when you will get tired of living that way – moving through life like a zombie reacting to the world instead of creating something different – a life of awareness, beauty, abundance, wonder, joy, vitality, and positive excitement.

The time will come when you will realize that your past experiences are just that – experiences. That they do not define you, do not dictate to you what you should fear and what you should crave. You have the power to decide who you want to be and what you want to experience each moment of your life.

You have the power to stop being a slave to your conditioned behavior which forces you to react in a habitual conditioned way. You can stop the vicious circle of repeated mistakes which attract the same drama into your life over and over again.

You can decide right now that you don't need them – that you don't need the drama and that it is not who you are anymore.

Action Steps

- Imagine your life without the drama. What would it be like? Is it a welcomed sensation?
- Since we cannot experience anything that we cannot first imagine, by imagining your life without drama and what it will feel like, you will take the most important step towards creating it.

CHAPTER 58

JUST BE YOURSELF

We are so busy playing different roles, defined by others and by our own ideas of who we should be and how we should behave, that when someone says, "just be yourself," we don't know what it means and how to do it.

"Just be yourself," is one of those things that is easier said than done and here is why…

You are not supposed to *try* and do something to be yourself because that will only be a new role you are choosing to play.

If you don't know what it means to be yourself and, at the same time, you are comfortable with that feeling, it means you are able to release all expectations of what it means and allow yourself to just BE.

When you allow yourself to just BE, to live without expectations of yourself, others, and how life should flow, you open up to the endless possibilities of your true self and allow that higher self to guide you in living your authentic life.

This authentic life is always for your greater good. So let go of trying to control it and to manipulate it thinking that you, as in your mind and your ego, know better.

"Just be yourself," means allowing yourself to be undefined and free. Be fully present at each moment, trusting that what is happening at this moment is your creation and serves a purpose regardless if we are consciously aware of it or not.

"It takes a lot of effort to be a person. It takes no effort to be yourself." Mooji

Action Steps

- You are already yourself.
- You don't need to attend trainings, do exercises, and try to change yourself in any way to be who you already are.
- *Become comfortable with not knowing. Become comfortable with not doing. Allow yourself to go with the flow, and to appreciate every moment you are blessed to be here.*

CHAPTER 59

RELEASING GUILT

Guilt prevents us from moving forward. It is our comfort zone – a familiar feeling that asks, "Who are you to do this and that, to become successful, to deserve better than what you have, to be loved and to be happy?"

Guilt is often a habitual reaction, which means we would often manifest situations which make us feel guilty. In this case, the pattern most likely has started in our childhood by well-meaning parents who thought that the best way to get what they wanted from their kids was to manipulate them with guilt.

There was a time when I felt guilty for everything, even if it rained! I also observed that most people live their lives with a burden of guilt – some heavier than others but most of us carry guilt around.

Fortunately, I have found people who do not feel guilty and do not allow the emotion of guilt to take permanent residence in their mind. When I asked them how they manage to do it, the basic belief behind a guilt-free mindset is this:

As long as everything is done with love and positive intent, and doesn't hurt anyone in the process, nothing is wrong and there is no need to feel guilty.

It took me some time to adopt the above formula as a way of life but eventually I succeeded and managed to reprogram myself, and so can you.

Release yourself from the prison of guilt and watch your life transform.

Action Steps

- If you have a habit or a pattern of feeling guilty, become aware of it and find a way to release it.
- You can do it through affirmations such as, "I no longer feel guilty"; "I no longer take responsibility for the happiness of the other person"; "No one has the power to make me feel guilty unless I let them"; "I love myself enough to let go of guilt."
- You can also use one of the tools provided in the Appendixes at the end of the book or seek professional help where you can access your subconscious through hypnosis, EFT, or other effective methods.

CHAPTER 60

AWARENESS DOESN'T ALWAYS PRODUCE THE RESULTS

It took me a long time to realize that just by wanting to change something and consciously doing all that I can to change it, more often than not, has only produced temporary results.

Unfortunately, some programming is so deeply ingrained and so deeply buried in our subconscious, that no amount of conscious effort can create change. No amount of willpower and practical knowledge will help to change the programming until the subconscious is accessed and the programming is rewritten.

For example, if your relationship has been hitting the same wall and you have been getting frustrated about the same things, then it is obvious that by fighting it and forcing things to change, you will not get the results that you want. The same thing goes for financial rollercoasters, weight yo-yoing, people letting you down, and so on.

One of the things that can help is understanding of what created a particular issue for you in the first place. When did it start? What is triggering it?

What kind of program in your subconscious are you running to manifest your experiences over and over again?

> ### Action Steps
>
> - To get the answers to the above questions, you will need to access your subconscious, a place where we store everything that has ever happened to us but do not remember all of it.
> - As mentioned above, there are many different ways to access subconscious, some of the most common are through meditation, through hypnotherapy, and through tapping. It makes sense to explore different ways and choose which work best for you.

CHAPTER 61

LIFE WITHOUT CHALLENGES

Think for a moment about your favorite movies or novels. In fact, think for a moment about every novel or movie that has ever interested you. What do they all have in common?

Every good storyline has one thing in common – the main character faces an adversity early on and throughout the story finds a way to overcome it. If there were no adversities or challenges, how interesting would the movie or a novel be?

After working with hundreds of people, there is something else that I found is very common – the answer to the question of what people consider their peak experiences. Besides giving birth to a baby or holding your own baby for the first time, an overwhelming majority of people describe the moments of triumph when they managed to overcome their greatest adversities.

This means that challenges and struggles are not only our greatest teachers, but without them life would basically be pretty boring, just like a movie where nothing really changes.

Subconsciously, we understand that and often, when all is calm and going smoothly in our life, we tend to create problems to spice up our life. We want to challenge ourselves, we want to achieve and overcome, we want to feel capable, valued, and deserving.

Action Steps

- When challenges and adversities appear in your life, welcome them and use them to expand, to grow, and to learn your next lesson.
- Remind yourself that you are resourceful enough and capable enough and that every storm eventually is replaced by sunshine.
- How soon you will see that sunshine depends on how well you can embrace and appreciate the moment as IS rather than reject it and fight it, wishing for things to be different.

CHAPTER 62

HOW TO BREAK THE PATTERN OF A PERSISTENT EMOTION

My friend, whose boyfriend suddenly stopped calling or writing to her, was feeling down and confused. On the third day I asked her if he had reappeared, and she said, "No." I suggested that she send a message to see if he was ok, to which she replied, "I need a bit more time to wallow in the emotion of being abandoned!"

Then we both laughed and the whole incident was no longer sad, disappointing, or even important. There was no more blame or confusion. It was suddenly perfectly clear – she needed to experience being abandoned, once again, and therefore, once again, someone appeared in her life to fulfil that wish.

It might be interesting to explore why she wanted to experience that feeling; whether it was self-punishment based on the feelings of guilt or shame, or possibly a childhood trauma reliving itself because it was never released, or self-sabotage based on low self-esteem and not feeling worthy, or possibly fear of being loved. However, I want to focus here on something else.

It is something that can help you take the first step towards taking responsibility for how you feel, and therefore, allow you to be in control and to transform unwanted emotions, and eliminate feelings of helplessness, self-criticism, judgement and blame.

What this experience taught me is that *every emotion we want to experience, will create circumstances that will allow us to experience it*. It will also bring into it the people who will act accordingly and consistently to manifest that emotion over and over again until we have had enough and want to create it differently.

Action Steps

To break the pattern of a persistent emotion continuing to resurface, take the following steps:

- Think of the negative emotion that is repeatedly manifesting in your life. Is it frustration? Impatience? Disappointment? Anger? Abandonment? Or possibly something else?
- This emotion, which was triggered by a dramatic event at some point in your life, and then got stuck in your energetic field, has been trying to break free by creating situations in your life that would bring your attention to it. So, your second step is to start noticing this emotion in a different way when it comes again.
- Your next step is to divert your attention from the person or circumstance that triggered it, to the emotion itself. It is not about the inappropriate or hurtful behavior of others, but about you needing to feel this emotion in order to release it.
- Once you can take responsibility for feeling what you are feeling, moving away from blame and lack of control, choose the emotional release tool from the Appendix that works best for you and free this emotion once and for all.

CHAPTER 63

DEALING WITH AN EMOTIONAL CRISIS

How many emotions throughout your lifetime have you chosen not to express, to push aside, or to bury either because you were taught to avoid conflict, did not know how to deal with those emotions, or were not ready to deal with those emotions?

How many patterns of resistance have you created in the process to keep those emotions well-hidden or to push them right back, when from time-to-time they would come to the surface, giving you an opportunity to release them?

Every one of us has spent years creating destructive patterns, burying unwanted emotions, and living in the illusion of the ego-driven reality and we cannot and should not expect to change it all at once.

So when all the work that you do on yourself, all the releasing, forgiving, accepting, and allowing, at times seems fruitless because you suddenly stumble on yet another big emotional crisis, remember this.

There are layers of patterns and emotions and most of us get to release them layer by layer. So, like with everything else, never give up or despair or feel that all that you do is futile, because it is not.

Every negative emotion released, every unwanted habit and pattern transformed, every situation that is fully accepted and loved – all bring you closer to your natural way of being – to the natural flow of well-being and joy as well as love and peace of mind.

When an emotional crisis comes up, just let it be. Don't fight it and don't feel bad for feeling it. In fact, be grateful that yet another emotion is ready to come to the surface for you to face, to learn from, and to let go.

It takes courage to come face-to-face with unwanted emotions and to take responsibility for them.

Action Steps

- If you are reading this book and have come this far, I have no doubt that you have that courage and you can and will get to that place of peace and love or any other emotional state to which your higher self is leading you right now.

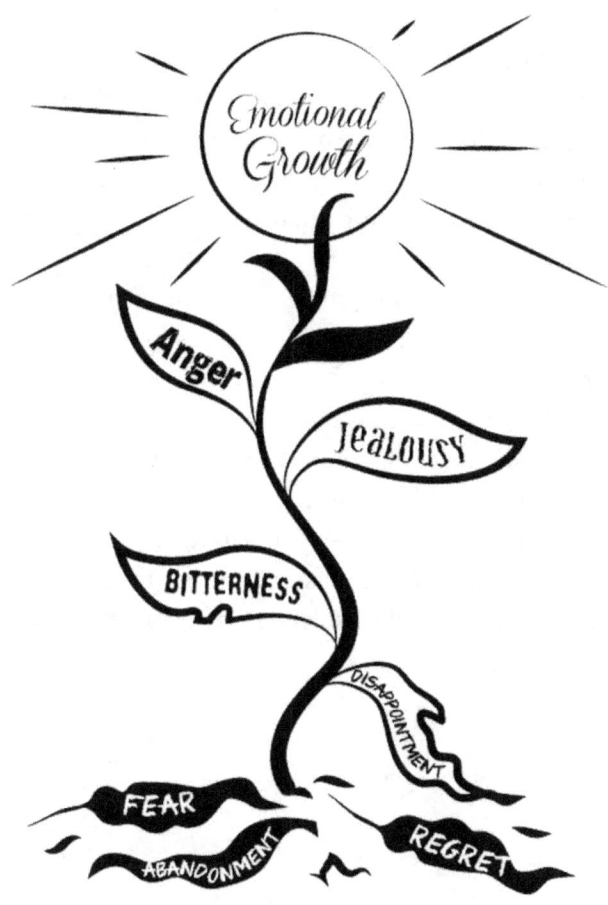

CHAPTER 64

BE THE LIGHT

When the same painful situation repeats itself over and over again; when the same person treats you unfairly over and over again; when we keep hitting the same wall and no amount of struggle, explaining, screaming, crying and praying seems to make a lasting difference, it is time to face the truth – these painful experiences that cause us suffering and even despair are our own manifestations based on our own resistance to *what is* and to the flow of life.

You can spend hours, days, even the rest of your life defending your righteousness and pointing to the unfairness of what is happening and how it is causing you pain but it will not make it any better and very unlikely that it will ever change. In fact, the more energy that we put into the situation, the more likely it will persist.

What if, instead of swimming in self-pity and negativity we use it as a signal to remind us to be less judgmental and resentful, and more forgiving, humble, and accepting?

The cycle of action and reaction can only be broken when the unconscious behavior of another dissolves or passes through us without attaching itself or hitting the inner wall of resistance and non-acceptance.

Accepting the situation as is doesn't mean justifying someone's dysfunctional behavior, it means being an observer rather than a reactor – bringing in the light where darkness will dissolve rather than fighting the darkness by becoming one with it.

Action Steps

- Next time you feel you are being attacked, or a difficult and negative situation arises once again, let it pass through you, resist the urge to rebuff and to defend – become the kind of space of inner peace and tranquility where anything that is not peace just disappears into it as if it never existed. This will remove the energy charge from this particular situation and will diminish its effect on you in the future, eventually changing and disappearing all together.
- Darkness disappears where there is light. Someone else's darkness can only attach itself to the darkness in you. If all you have inside is light, no one and nothing can hurt you.
- BE THE LIGHT.

CHAPTER 65

PATIENCE IS A VIRTUE

One of the hardest things for me to learn has been patience. Like most people, I want to see the results of my efforts as soon as possible and make things happen when I want them to happen.

When I get impatient, I remind myself that I am part of the creation just like everything else around me and I need to follow the same rules, which require patience. It takes time for the fetus to develop, for the flower to bloom, and for the fruit to ripen. It also takes time for the seeds that we plant to achieve our success to bloom and to show their fruits.

So, using nature as a guide to achieving lasting change, before you plant new seeds in your garden, take the time to get rid of all the 'weeds' by letting go of everything and everyone in the past that are making your garden ugly, and only then plant the seeds into the clean fertile grounds.

Sure we want to see beautiful flowers or fruits and vegetables as soon as we plant them, but we wait patiently for nature to take its course. It is the same kind of patience that is necessary to grow the new wonderful experiences in our lives without the fear of being suffocated by the weeds of yesterday.

"Inner transformation cannot be seen as it occurs. The brain shifts as the person shifts. The brain has no way of preserving its old pathways once new ones have been created." Deepak Chopra

Even though we cannot see the inner work and transformation, when it does happen, there is no going back. Once you truly let go of the past or the emotions that were stuck and were holding you back, you create new pathways for a new and brighter future.

Action Steps

- Sometimes transformation happens spontaneously, but that is very rare, most of the time we need to be patient and allow the process to unfold, trusting that when we live each moment with gratitude, acceptance, and joy in the present, we are planting the seeds that will eventually manifest more of the same as our life unfolds.

"Adopt the pace of nature: her secret is patience." Ralf Waldo Emerson

PART 5

CONCLUSION

CHAPTER 66

THE DANCE OF LIFE

Have you ever tried to learn a new dance?

After my first ballroom class I remember coming home completely demoralized. I couldn't figure out how I could think about moving in rhythm, pointing my toes in one place and flexing in another, keeping my knees straight when they needed to be straight, which didn't mean all the time, keeping my back very straight and my body bent slightly forward...all that and more while somehow not looking like some spasmodic constipated robot.

And yet, when I looked at more advanced couples, who effortlessly glided on the dance floor looking suave, confident, sexy, and beautiful, I realized that there was a time when they felt what I felt and moved as I moved.

Some very lucky people have an inborn talent for dancing, for singing, for certain sports or academics; however most of us, and even those who are talented, have to spend hours and hours of working hard to achieve those effortless results we admire.

It is no different with mastering our emotions and our life.

It takes time. It takes effort. But when you get there... WOW! You just flow, and glide, and sway, in the most elegant and exciting way.

You get to attract and achieve amazing things, almost effortlessly. And only you know how hard you had to work to get there.

Action Steps

- Hard work pays off. Keep doing what you know you should be doing and you will reap the rewards.

CHAPTER 67

WHEN SH-T HAPPENS

When we understand that we create our reality and that reality presents us with difficult and painful experiences, there is a tendency to feel that somehow we have failed, that we did something wrong in this process of creation.

If you tend to be self-critical and give in to blaming yourself for feeling bad, even when you know it is counterproductive, then this might help…

When we make a conscious decision to change, our Higher Self gifts us opportunities to test what in theory we have decided to change.

It is not easy to change what has been habitually done for years, but once we manage to handle the situation in a new way, we know that the shift has taken place and the good news is – there is no going back.

However, sometimes we have to be faced with difficult experiences that trigger the old patterns a few times to get it right.

This is not a reason to panic, to feel inadequate or to get down. Just shake it off or, even better, laugh it off and tell yourself that next time you will do it differently.

Action Steps

- Do not look at what you consider negative experiences as some kind of failure or inability to create differently on your part.
- When you feel that you could have handled yourself better, just replay the scenario in your head and imagine how you would have preferred to react.
- Feel it. Replay the positive scenario in your head a few times. This will help you to manifest it at the next opportunity. And that opportunity will eventually and inevitable come.

CHAPTER 68

THE DANGER OF DESIRE

"*Too much intention creates tension.*" Mooji

I have been fortunate to meet and to speak to a number of enlightened Beings. Just to sit next to them or even to be in the same room with them raised my vibration and made me feel calmer, more peaceful, and more appreciative of everything.

Coming into their vibrational frequency was enough to promote my personal growth; however, years of conditioning of operating on a mental level prompted me to ask many questions, answers to which fascinated me and stirred an even greater desire to be more like them.

It is not until later that I have come to a realization – *desire* is what has kept me from just being that enlightened person, has kept me from seeing that same light within myself and allowing it to shine.

The desire meant that I didn't feel I had enough knowledge, or experience, or wisdom; made me feel that I wasn't being enough to be an enlightened person.

And so the danger of desire is that it implies that something is keeping us from just being that person or from having what we want or from doing what we want.

Desire implies lack of what we want and in that vibration of lack it keeps it away from us – keeping it stuck as desire rather than an experience.

Action Steps

- Think of something that you have desired for some time.
- Now feel what it would feel like to have it – really feel it!
- Every time this desire resurfaces, imagine, feel and act *as if it has already happened*.
- What you feel at this moment is what creates your reality. The more you feel lack through desire, the more it will stay that way; *the more you feel the happiness of experiencing what you desire as it is already happened, the faster it will become your reality.*

CHAPTER 69

THE IMPORTANCE OF HUMILITY

What does it really mean to be humble? And why is it such an important emotional state to reach?

The term *humility* comes from the Latin word *humilis* which means "grounded" or "from the earth."

Being humble, down to earth, and removing importance from your ego-driven identity helps you become one with the universe and to be your authentic powerful self.

It is important to understand that humility does not mean thinking low of yourself, making yourself less than others and diminishing your achievements or talents. On the contrary.

Rabbi Lord Jonathan Sacks states that humility is *"An appreciation of oneself, one's talents, skills, and virtues."* It means to *"appreciate the self that one has received…and in recognition of the mysteries and complexities of life, one becomes humbled to the awesomeness one is and what one can achieve."*

Humility also means to appreciate the worthiness of others, seeing everyone as important or equal to yourself as well as the ability to recognize our insignificance in the vastness of the universe, at the same time, seeing ourselves as creators of our universe.

Finally, the greatest expression of humility comes in our ability to live up to our greatest inborn potential, beyond our own needs and desires and in the service of others.

Action Steps

- Not being driven by the false desires and fears of the ego and aligning yourself with your true powerful self, helps you manifest your higher purpose in a natural and easy way.
- Stop feeding your ego by demanding (often subconsciously) attention and recognition for your deeds and achievements and watch your life transform into a much more peaceful, contented, and joyful space to be in.

CHAPTER 70

THE FORMULA FOR LIVING A GOOD LIFE

There is a difference between making a living and making a life.

The formula for living a good life is pretty simple – where you channel your focus is what you experience and what determines the quality of life that you are living.

Your emotions, at every moment, are indicating to you where the flow of your attention is going. If the feelings you are experiencing are unpleasant, you are not being congruent with your true self and most likely feeling disconnected and scared.

If you are feeling content, peaceful and loving, then you know that at this moment you are moving with the flow of life creating more experiences where these positive, feel-good emotion dominate.

The Formula for Living a Good Life | 151

Action Steps

- Always take responsibility for all that is happening in your life and remind yourself that YOU are the creator of it.
- Allow the unwanted thoughts to flow by without feeding them your energy.
- Imagine your ideal life often, feeling what it would feel like.
- You are creating at this moment and at every moment. Create wisely.

CONCLUSION
TOMORROW IS PROMISED TO NO ONE

So what do you choose for yourself? How would you like to live and what emotions would you like to experience for the rest of your life?

Tomorrow is promised to no one. I believe that even if I had just one more day to live, I would want to live it on my terms, in the happiest possible way, being the best I can be and seeing the beauty in everyone around me. And if I am fortunate to be gifted another day of life after that, I want to live it just the same.

I committed some time ago to live my life to the fullest, one day at a time, believing that no matter what it brings me, it is somehow and always for the better; that every day is a blessing and an opportunity to learn, to grow, to be around those we love, to explore and to expand… To become, or more likely, to remind myself, of who I truly am and to be that person by shedding and releasing fear-based emotions, beliefs and thoughts that have been holding me back.

Everyone deserves to do what they love and to live their life on their terms.

You have suffered enough, you have paid for your mistakes, it is time to end your struggles and to realize that it is YOUR TURN – to step under the flow of well-being and to allow it to shower you with all that is good and wonderful and wash away your feelings of guilt and suffering. Let it fill you with light and happiness and unconditional love.

It is time for you to banish your doubts and to take the central stage and be the beneficiary of positive abundance in all areas of your life.

It's your turn to feel and to be blessed, to live YOUR life – the life you always wanted and deserve to live, creating your own fulfilling reality and be the person you always wanted to be.

> **Action Steps**
> - *To feel is to be alive. To be alive is a blessing.*
> - Even when the emotion you are currently experiencing is unpleasant, remember that it is helping you to move towards, and to align yourself with, your higher self.
> - Appreciate *every* emotion, every moment as a gift and a chance to experience fully the life that you are now consciously creating.

APPENDIX I

TEN BASIC STEPS FOR RELEASING EMOTIONS

1. **Stop judging** (yourself, the other person, or the situation).
2. **Accept the situation** for what it is and **take responsibility** for it.
3. **Allow yourself to feel** what you are feeling – observe the emotion as something that is outside of you, get curious about the emotion and know that when you are ready and when you want to, you can release it and send it on its way.
4. It is not always necessary to analyze why you feel what you feel. **Just let the emotion pass through you** without giving it too much thought or too much attention.
5. **Release the emotion** on all levels, choose what works best for you:
    a. Scream as loud as you can (not at someone, just into a space);
    b. Punch a punching bag, a pillow, or just the air;
    c. Shake your body starting at your feet and then all the way up;
    d. Go to the gym or take a vigorous fitness class such as kick boxing;
    e. Go for a run;
    f. Do yoga;
    g. Go into nature;
    h. Sit under a tree;
    i. Use visualization, imagining the emotion transforming itself and leaving your body as a dark liquid, or as some animal, or as some cartoon character, or anything else that comes to your imagination;
    j. Allow yourself to cry – for example, take a long bath with candles, put the music you like and allow yourself to cry until no more tears left;
    k. Pray;
    l. Do breathing exercises;
    m. Research and find other ways that work well for you.
6. **Forgive yourself**.
7. **Give yourself time to heal**.
8. **Ask for help** if the emotion is persistent. Some emotions are too deeply ingrained and the cause of them cannot be understood on a conscious level. In this case, professional help is highly advisable.

9. **Release all emotions on a daily basis** before going to sleep so that they do not accumulate and become powerful. Just go through the main episodes of your day and breath out the emotions associated with all that has happened.
10. **Feel gratitude** towards yourself for loving yourself enough to take care of your needs, of your happiness and well-being, and for taking the time to do what needs to be done in order to live your best life.

APPENDIX II

HOLISTIC APPROACH TO IDENTIFYING AND RELEASING FIVE MOST COMMON UNWANTED EMOTIONS

by Lesley Lois Parry

Lesley Lois Parry is one of my favorite gurus, teachers, and therapists, for over a decade now, who has also become a close friend of mine. She is a fully qualified Holistic Practitioner (MFHT IIHHT) with over 30 years' experience working with and supporting on a professional and personal basis Doctor's, Neuroscientist's, Chiropractor's, CEO's, Artist's, Therapist's ,Life Coaches, Celebrities, Hypnotherapist's, Families/individuals of alcoholism, Soldiers/PTSD, Bereavement, Terminal illness, Children, Pregnancy/Fertility, and Animals.

Lesley has developed ERA (Emotional Release Ad-Infinitum), a technique which finds and releases blocked emotions in minutes and once released, they do not come back.

For more information, please email: lesleylewisparry@hotmail.com or visit www.ERAtherapy.com

Lesley has kindly agreed to share her knowledge on releasing five most commonly unwanted emotions with us:

ANGER

Anger is a very normal response when '*perceived boundaries have been crossed*' that intimate some kind of danger, real or imagined, when we feel that we are not in control.

Anger is held in the *liver/gallbladder* and *thighs*. It is felt in the tendons and neck and can lead to the following **physical manifestations:**

- Arthritis
- Dry Eyes
- Gall Stones

Holistic Approach to Identifying and Releasing | 157

- Headaches/Migraines
- High Blood Pressure
- Hormonal Imbalances
- Inflexibility of Movement/Stiffness/Joint Pain
- Liver Problems
- Osteoarthritis
- Restless Leg Syndrome
- Rib Pain
- Spasms
- Watering Eyes
- Anger Outbursts/Aggression/Confrontation
- Depression
- Feeling Stuck
- Frustration
- Hate/Resentment
- Impulsive/Erratic Behavior
- Indecision
- Inflexibility
- Pensive
- Poor judgement
- Reckless
- Tyrannical

Stress Reaction: Being controlling.

Remedies

- Shout whilst holding middle finger. This will develop acceptance which when balanced will lead to patience. If shouting is not appropriate, just squeeze the middle finger when a wave of anger comes.
- Wear or surround yourself with the color green.
- Meditate and use Aromatherapy Oils to reduce anger such as *Lavender, Ylang Ylang, Roman Chamomile, Myrrh, Bergamot,* and *Orange*.
- Use Bach Flower Essences any time you feel the need such as *Cherry Plum* when you feel like you will explode. *Holly* for jealousy. *Willow* for when

you feel sorry for yourself or can't accept something. *Heather* for when you are lonely and need to talk. *Beech* when you focus on others faults and are critical.
- The eyes are affected by anger. What we do not want to see or acknowledge in our future, present or what has already past. Reading is an excellent way of refocusing your attention in the present moment, bringing some relief.

SORROW/SADNESS

It is a very normal response to feel deep sadness or sorrow when we lose someone or something that used to bring us love and joy. Acceptance can be difficult when we find ourselves confronted with this kind of change in life circumstances.

Sorrow is held in the *heart* and *small intestines*. It is felt in the hands and chest and can lead to emotional imbalances in the heart and an inability to express joy and happiness as the result of emotional shock or trauma.

Some Physical Manifestations can be

- Anxiety/Sense of dread
- Arteriosclerosis
- Heart disease
- Insomnia/Disturbing dreams
- Irregular heartbeat
- Mouth sores/Tongue sores/Ulcers
- Palpitations
- Poor Memory
- Stroke
- Stuttering
- You may become excitable, selfish and self-centered, become flirtatious for attention and have grandiose ideas to fill the emptiness that you feel.
- Addictions/Cravings for stimulation
- Fluctuations in emotion/High and low feelings
- Inability to love or feel love/Numbness
- Insulted easily
- Nervous

- Sexually overstimulated
- Unfinished projects
- Unfulfilled

Stress Reaction: Sadness.

Remedies

- Walk whilst squeezing the little finger. This will develop peace and when balanced will lead to joyfulness.
- Wear or surround yourself with the color red.
- Meditate and use Aromatherapy Oils such as *Bergamot, Roman Chamomile, Juniper, and Lavender*.
- Bach Flower Essences such as *Mustard* for when you are sad without a reason. *Elm* for overwhelm. *Sweet Chestnut* when sorrow is unbearable and you have reached the limit of your endurance. *Willow* for when you feel sorry for yourself after suffering adversity. *Gorse* for hopelessness. *Gentian* for when you are easily discouraged after a small setback, skeptical or pessimistic. *Larch* for lack of self-confidence and self-esteem.
- As the tongue is used for the sense of taste, eating honey and healthy sweet foods like red bell pepper, melon, strawberries, raspberries, tomatoes, cherries, beetroot will sweeten life a little whilst the sadness and sorrow moves through you. Stay away from sugar and chocolate.

WORRY

Worry is held in the *spleen* and *stomach* and is associated with not feeling grounded or connected. It is felt in the pancreas and muscles and can lead to eating disorders and an inability to take in nourishment and transform food and fluids leading to congestion and insulin resistance, a pre-diabetic condition.

Physical Conditions can be

- Anorexia
- Bulimia
- Craving Sweets

- Diabetes
- Hypoglycemia
- Nausea
- Overeating
- Stomach issues
- Weak muscles
- Weight gain
- Ambivalence
- Clinging
- Interfering
- Joyless, inability to feel joy
- Lack of sympathy/Inability to nurture others
- Martyrdom/Self-sacrifice
- Obsessing
- Over Bearing/Smothering

Stress reaction: Stubbornness.

Remedies

- Sit down whilst squeezing your thumb and sing. This will develop empathy and when balanced will lead to trust. If not appropriate to sing then squeeze thumb when overcome with worry.
- Wear or surround yourself with the color yellow or brown.
- Meditate and use Aromatherapy Oils to reduce worry such as *Bergamot, Basil, Clary, Sage, Frankincense, Lavender, Marjoram, Palmarosa, Ylang Ylang*.
- Bach Flower Essences – *Aspen* for unknown worry, gloom and doom or evil forebodings. *Cherry Plum* for over-reacting or feeling out of control, impatiens for nervousness, irritability, and over reaction. *Mimulus* for known fears/concerns such as illness, natural disasters, heights, drawing, abuse, small spaces, financial ruin, abandonment, failure, success. *Red Chestnut* for fretting, obsessiveness over wellbeing of loved ones. *Rock Rose* for hysteria, panic, paranoia, fright. *White Chestnut* for mental replaying of event real or imagined, reliving the past, being stuck in the head.

- The mouth is used for taking in nourishment and sensing the different textures of food. Allowing the different textures that life has to offer with grace will ease any worries and reduce the duration and frequency over time.

GRIEF

Grief is a very normal response to loss whether it is a loved one, a home, a marriage, a business or an expectation of life.

It is held in the *lungs* and *large intestines* and only when one cannot move through the normal phases of grief does it result as a problem. It is felt in the skin and shoulders and can lead to breathing difficulties, skin eruptions and digestive disorders.

Some Physical Manifestations can be

- Asthma/Lung disorders/Bronchitis
- Constipation, IBS
- Colitis/Diverticulitis
- Immune system disorders
- Large intestine disorders
- Sinus problems

Character Changes

- It will be hard for you to express yourself fully. You may become aloof in relationships. Hypocrisy can replace integrity. Disappointment and self-doubt can take over leading to subordination in situations and relationships. It is difficult to let go of past hurts and losses.
- Low self-esteem
- No personal boundaries/Spiritual belief
- Obsessive Compulsive Disorder
- Perfectionism
- Problems with intimacy and authority
- Self-righteousness

Stress reaction: Coughing.

Remedies

- Lie down whilst squeezing your ring finger and cry. This will develop confidence and when balanced will lead to happiness. If lying down and crying is not appropriate squeeze the ring finger when a wave of sadness comes.
- Wear or surround yourself with the color white.
- Meditate and use Aromatherapy Oils such as *Neroli, Frankincense, Lavender, Rose, Melissa, Bergamot*.
- Bach Flower Essences any time you feel the need such as Rescue Remedy to restore calm and reduce panic. *Water Violet* brings feelings to the forefront. *Honeysuckle* for moving on. *Gorse* to restore hope. *Gentian* for when you have lost faith. *Olive* for exhaustion after long illness. *Hornbeam* restores enthusiasm for life. *Star of Bethlehem* for shock, numbness brought on by trauma. *Elm* for overwhelm.
- As the nose and the sense of smell is affected by grief, the above oils and essences are uniquely qualified to help balance and restore the emotions in times of grief.

FEAR

Fear is a very normal response to anything that we believe consciously or unconsciously threatens our life. When we are faced with death, birth or changing the way we are expressing our uniqueness in life, we may need a period of hibernation, quiet time and pulling back. Fear is a normal response that helps us to do this if allowed to unfold naturally.

Fear is held in the *kidneys* and *bladder*. It is felt in the knees and low back and if blocked from fully expressing itself can lead to trembling, exhaustion, isolation and absent-mindedness.

Some Physical Manifestations could be

- Adrenal fatigue
- Dark circles under eyes/Puffiness
- Hair thinning/Loss of hair/Premature greying

- Heel pain/Knee pain
- Hormonal imbalance
- Hypothyroidism
- Impotence/Infertility/Lack of libido
- Kidney disease/Kidney stones
- Lower back pain
- Tinnitus/Ringing in the ears
- Urinary Tract Infection
- It will be difficult for you to be resilient during everyday life and vitality and endurance are severely compromised.
- Panic Attacks/Anxiety attacks
- Phobias
- Detachment
- Extreme exhaustion/No vitality or endurance

Stress Reaction: Trembling.

Remedies

- Stand whilst squeezing the Index finger and groan. This will create balance reducing the feeling of fear and lead to courage. If standing and groaning is not appropriate, squeeze the Index finger when you feel a wave of fear.
- Wear or surround yourself with the color blue or black.
- Meditate and use Aromatherapy Oils to calm fear such as *Sandalwood, Cypress, Lemon, Bergamot, Orange, Cedarwood, Neroli, Basil.*
- Bach Flower Essences any time you feel the need such as *Rock Rose* for terror or fright. *Mimulus* for the type of fear you can't put a name on such as reasons for shyness, being alone, losing a job. *Cherry Plum* for fear of losing control of thoughts and actions, doing things that are bad for oneself – teaches trust in one's spontaneous wisdom and courage to follow your path. *Aspen* for unexplained vague fear. *Red Chestnut* for anxiety over loved ones.
- As the ears and the sense of sound is affected by fear then playing calming and pleasing music will also help balance and restore the emotions in fearful times.

ABOUT THE ARTIST

Anna Polonsky is a Florida based multimedia artist who explores the realm of imagination in both digital and traditional mediums. Her skills range from graphic design and vector illustrations to traditional paintings and sculptures. As a passionate visual content creator, she has taken on challenging projects and has worked with clients from all around the world, across a wide array of industries such as architecture, entertainment, manufacturing and more. Anna is driven by the vision of creating works of art that will encourage artists and non-artists alike to open their minds toward the realm of imagination and the power of thought.

Working with Masha on this incredibly empowering publication has truly made a positive impact on Anna's art, helping her to create every image in this book into something that will inspire others.

To contact Anna please write to: polonskyart@gmail.com or visit www.annapolonskyart.com

ABOUT THE AUTHOR

Masha Malka is a Russian/American who spends her time living between Sunny Isles, Florida and Marbella, Spain. She is a best-selling author and founder of The One Minute Coach™ educational system. She has worked as an executive coach for over 15 years; built a successful import and distribution company; taught Business Leadership at MUIC; won Ballroom competitions; got her Master's Degree in Higher Education while raising three children. Masha also has training certificates in Accelerated Learning Techniques and Transformational Thinking, Graduate Certificate in Teaching and Training Online and a diploma in Clinical Hypnotherapy. She is an author of *Discover Your Inborn Genius e-book*; a contributing author to the *Chicken Soup for the Soul: Power Moms*; the *Power of Persistence* book; *Achieve Your Ultimate Success* DVD, and much more.

The experiences of overcoming the struggles of being a refugee at 17 years old, dealing with a very difficult break-up of a 20-year marriage, living in seven countries, coaching hundreds of people around the world and constantly learning, researching and applying her knowledge, have all made this book possible.

To learn more about Masha Malka and her programs, please visit www.mashamalka.com

PERSONAL MESSAGE

Thank you for your dedication to your happiness and well-being, for investing your time to read this book, and for connecting to me through this pages!

To help you on your continuous journey of learning, I have joined forces with some very talented avant-garde people to develop an educational/coaching application for smart phones which allows you to have a mentor-on-the-go, to implement the knowledge, to connect with like-minded people and receive advice and feedback from peers and mentors.

Please take a moment to visit
www.theoneminutecoachapp.com

There are special gifts for my readers with the **gift code**: ilikemyself

You will also be able to send me a direct message through the app, so hope to hear from you soon!

With love and gratitude

www.ingramcontent.com/pod-product-compliance
Lightning Source LLC
Chambersburg PA
CBHW071621080526
44588CB00010B/1212